EXPLORERS
EXTRAORDINARY

EXPLORERS
EXTRAORDINARY
John Keay

JEREMY P. TARCHER, INC.
Los Angeles
Distributed by St. Martin's Press
New York

Library of Congress Cataloging-in-Publication Data

Keay, John.
    Explorers extraordinary.

    Bibliography: p.
    1. Explorers — Biography.   I. Title.
G200.E355   1986   910′.92′2   [B]   86-14333
ISBN 0-87477-397-0 (pbk.)

Jeremy P. Tarcher, Inc.
9110 Sunset Blvd.
Los Angeles, CA 90069
Typeset by Rowland Phototypesetting Ltd,
Bury St Edmunds, Suffolk, Great Britain

Manufactured in the United States of America
10 9 8 7 6 5 4 3 2 1

For my sister, Pat

CONTENTS

ILLUSTRATIONS

INTRODUCTION

Except that they are all curiosities, the heroes of this book have practically nothing in common. Like those in *Eccentric Travellers* they represent a purely personal choice. Three – Cochrane, de Rougemont and Savage Landor – have not been the subject of biographies and therefore seem especially worthy of attention. No less does that lovable canoeist John MacGregor, whose books are surely long overdue for reprinting and whose biography is extremely hard to find.

Perhaps because of their sex, Mary Kingsley and Isabelle Eberhardt are better known. So, because of his considerable achievement, is the impossible Ludwig Leichhardt. Yet in all three cases their biographies are long out of print and reappraisal seems justified.

All this, though, is by way of pretext. The choice, as I say, is personal; they are simply characters to whom I took a fancy. Subsequently I became equally intrigued by their narratives. It seemed that these yarns from the periphery of the great nineteenth-century travel writing tradition could be taken as some sort of commentary on the conventions of the genre and on its decline towards the end of the century. I advance the idea with caution. It may simply be the chance outcome of a wholly random and unrepresentative selection. Yet can it be coincidence that a reading public seduced by the improbable tale of Louis de Rougemont was simultaneously hoodwinked by the terrible Savage Landor?

All these explorers – it is the job description they would have chosen – were acutely conscious of contributing to a literary tradition. They were inspired by books as much as places – and in one case, entirely by books. Cochrane modelled his philosophy of travel on that of Mungo Park; and MacGregor illustrated one of Livingstone's books and unconsciously parodied Speke's search for the source of the Nile. Savage Landor relished the heroics of Samuel Baker, Isabelle Eberhardt pined after the exotic romanticism of Pierre Loti. All travelled with the intention of writing about their travels and therefore with an eye to what they regarded as good travel book material.

'No one expects literature in a work of travel,' wrote Mary Kingsley; it was by way of apology for one of her grammatical extravaganzas. Yet they did expect entertainment and no one laid it on thicker than Miss Kingsley. Romance, excitement, novelty must be there. As Ludwig Leichhardt discovered, to go where white man never went before was simply not enough. You had to write about it, preferably convincingly, certainly entertainingly. And if white man had already been there before you, you had to pretend he had not, like Savage Landor, or do it differently, like John MacGregor, or make it up, like Louis de Rougemont.

How far the travel writer may reasonably go in these directions is as sensitive an issue today as it was in 1900. Heroics, it is true, we relish less; but a good laugh or a salacious encounter is most acceptable. The fact that today's travel writer may be at heart a novelist accustomed to a process of literary distillation that transposes incidents and produces composite locations peopled by exaggerated type figures only occasionally troubles our consciences.

In all good travel books there has to be a balance between authenticity and entertainment. Some of the characters in this book appear not to have achieved it. But it would never do to judge them too harshly. They are not the only ones.

EXPLORERS
EXTRAORDINARY

CHAPTER ONE
'ARMA VIRUMQUE CANOE'
John 'Rob Roy' MacGregor

The Working Men's Institute in London's Edgware Road was packed to capacity. Bills pasted to its bare cream walls promised a lecture about canoeing, a pastime in the 1870s enjoyed exclusively by aristocrats and savages. But the working men of Willesden and Paddington were not discouraged and neither were the working women and the working children. 'Old Rob Roy of the Ragged Schools' was the speaker; they wouldn't miss it for a music-hall. Preceded by a reputation for endearing buffoonery and accompanied by a whole cart-load of props, Rob Roy gave performances, not lectures.

On the evening of January 12, 1870 it fell to the Reverend Allon to introduce the distinguished speaker. Boxer, evangelist, marksman, traveller, philanthropist, and canoeist extraordinary, it was hard to do the man justice. But here he was, fresh from encounters with the Arabs and come to tell the working men of Willesden all about them, Mr John Mac-Gregor, alias Rob Roy. To a chorus of clapping and cockney catcalls up went the curtain and forward stepped a lanky gentleman with arms flailing. He was imitating the action of a canoeist's paddle. The canoe itself was centre stage, fully rigged – for it carried a sail – and sporting a blue silk ensign. Beside it was a potted plant, identified as papyrus, and a few stalks of corn, grown, according to MacGregor, from seed three thousand years old which he had found inside an Egyptian mummy. But he would come to these. First he should introduce the boat and its crew; or 'arma virumque canoe' as he quipped at more refined gatherings.

To every ship its galley and its cook; he delved inside the canoe and came out with a shoe bag containing minuscule stove, canteen, eggs and bacon, and an all-purpose piece of cutlery shaped like his paddle with fork prongs at one end and spoon at the other. He begged leave to draw his audience's kind attention to the pointed shape of the spoon; this ingenious feature meant that, though of tablespoon size, it could also be used for tackling a boiled egg. Next the medicine chest – he held up a matchbox containing sticking-plaster and quinine; and the ship's tailor – out came a cork stuck with twelve pins and a threaded needle plus one spare button. The ship's mascot? A small yapping dog of uncertain breed raced on stage and sat, figurehead-like, on the bow of the canoe. The dog, like his master and like the canoe, was called Rob Roy. Lastly and most important, the ship's chaplain. From his pocket he pulled a much thumbed Testament and from inside the stern of the canoe came a bundle of tracts. As he declaimed an appropriate verse from scripture, the tracts were passed amongst the audience. So much for the overture. MacGregor withdrew behind a screen.

He emerged in full canoeing attire – Norfolk jacket of red flannel (to be changed for one of sober grey when entering hostile waters) and a solar topi wrapped with a flowing turban to protect neck and back from sunstroke. Seated comfortably in the canoe, with waterproof sheeting buttoned to the Norfolk jacket, he began his story. The excitement was too much. The energy of his delivery being more than matched by a restless disposition, scarcely two sentences passed without some novel illustration.

In giving an amusing description of a long desert ride on camel-back [recalled an admirer] he would assume a scarlet tunic and turban and, mounting a chair which represented the camel's back and holding an umbrella of many colours, would depict the movements of a camel rider to the life and at the same time imitate the noises made by camels to express various emotions such as anger at being loaded or pleasure when drinking water. Then when describing the remote parts of the Nile about the hour of sunset he would imitate the noises of lions and the general chorus of animals of many kinds. When discoursing on mummies he would burn before the audience a small portion of mummy dust to demonstrate how largely creosote entered into the embalming material.

Mention of the Nile reminded him of his boy. A petulant Arab lad, he was on hand to supply a suitable musical accompaniment but could not be persuaded on stage. The working men of Willesden were encouraged to bawl for the reluctant Arab as MacGregor again dashed behind the screen. After an altercation in Arabic he reappeared in long white gelabiyeh with a hubble-bubble pipe and an instrument that looked like a biscuit box. Sitting cross-legged he puffed furiously on some evil-smelling tobacco. Then he intoned a guttural Arabic dirge and 'at the same time he assumed the postures and gestures of a Bedouin desert ranger'.

The performance ended, as it usually would, with the crocodile. Having told of how he encountered one of these creatures in a murky stream near Haifa, how it nearly had the *Rob Roy* canoe and its captain for breakfast, and how this was the only crocodile ever recorded in Palestine, the lights dimmed and MacGregor prepared for sleep. Strapping his bed to his back and donning a Greek nightcap, he climbed back into the canoe, rigged up his mosquito-net, lit his lamp, and appeared to doze off under a copy of *The Times*. Suddenly the howl of a jackal filled the darkened hall. The sleeping canoeist leapt from beneath *Times* and mosquito-net and jabbered dementedly. He had been having a nightmare about a gigantic crocodile. As he spoke, the very animal appeared on a large backcloth which unfurled behind him. MacGregor himself was depicted riding the brute with 'God Save the Queen' in one corner and 'Success to the Edgware Road Working Men's Institute' in the other. The lights went up, the applause rained forth, and the show was over.

For this performance repeated up and down the country at least once a week for several years MacGregor's fee was high, usually £50 or £100. But none of it did he pocket, not even expenses. The money stayed with the Working Men's Institutes and other charitable organisations that he chose to support. If they could raise the price of his fee, he would speak and they would benefit. The scheme, which eventually raised over £10,000, was as ingenious as the domestic arrangements on his canoe. And it gave MacGregor almost as much satisfaction. A man of juggernaut convictions, he knew

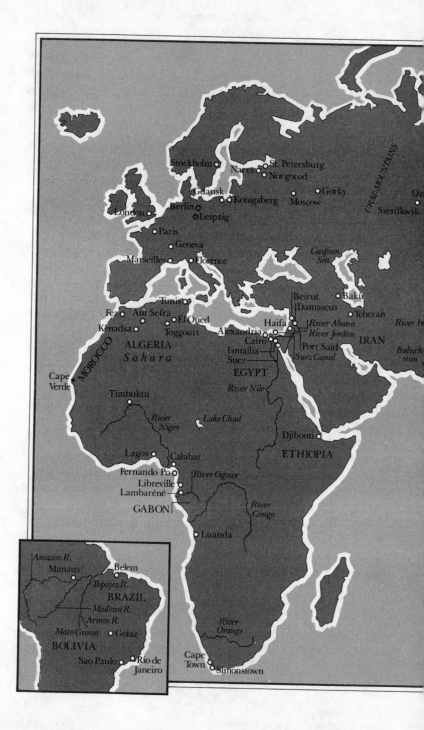

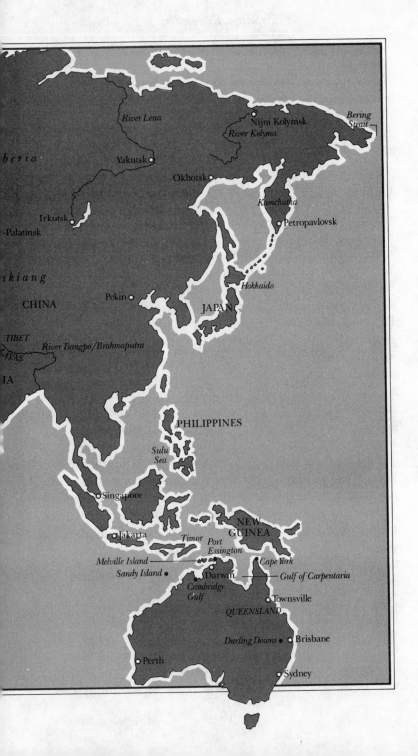

beyond all doubt that he had been singled out to serve his fellow men.

For to John MacGregor God had shown his hand in no uncertain way – or, in the more matter-of-fact words of the *Dictionary of National Biography*, 'adventures came to him early'. His father, an army major, and his mother had been sailing for India aboard the *Kent* when, close-reefed in a gale in the Bay of Biscay, she caught fire. Seven hundred crew and passengers prayed and panicked as the flames rose and the ship settled. Panic accounted for the speedy loss of three of the ship's six lifeboats; prayer brought the unhoped-for succour of a passing brig. In tumultuous seas over half the *Kent*'s complement were ferried to safety, among them Major and Mrs MacGregor, the latter, in spite of a ducking, still clutching her baby boy; he was thirty-five days old.

They watched the *Kent* go down, then faced a new trial. The brig was now so overcrowded that it was a case of standing-room only. For three days she wallowed towards Falmouth and for three days they stood. Throughout, baby John howled. To a nasty case of 'thrush' was added acute hunger, his mother's milk having dried up in the excitement. But he survived and it was, of course, a miracle. Thereafter John MacGregor had two birthdays: January 24, the anniversary of his first delivery, and March 1, the anniversary of his second.

Besides the comforting assurance of knowing that he had been 'chosen', MacGregor derived a number of more practical convictions from this early brush with the perils of the deep. Taking the muscular Christianity of his generation to extremes of evangelical body-building, he equated all that was physical, brave and vigorous with right-minded religion, and all that was weak, ignominious and fearful with heresy. Mishaps at sea clearly represented a fall from grace; the Royal National Lifeboat Institute thus became one of his most favoured charities and figured prominently in his lecture tours. Even more meritorious than the lifeboat was the lighthouse, for, as he noted in the margin of his Testament, the former saved those already shipwrecked but the latter prevented the shipwreck itself. He liked to see himself as a

1 John MacGregor in lecturing attire. The corn he holds was grown
from seed found inside an Egyptian mummy.

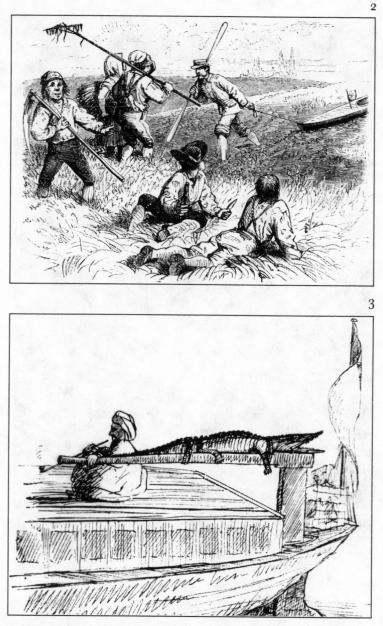

2 'A canoe voyage has its drawbacks'. MacGregor goes cross-country on the Upper Danube

3 MacGregor's first crocodile, shot on the Nile in 1850 and destined to adorn his study

lighthouse, a beacon of right-minded religion keeping his fellow men on the straight and narrow. But again parable and precept somehow got confused; he would take to paddling the *Rob Roy* out to spray-girt rocks, there to surprise unsuspecting lighthousemen with a parcel of tracts and tobacco.

To naval training ships, like the *Chichester* on the Thames, went the royalties from his books. Usually he attended their prize-givings and himself bestowed the so-called Rob Roy Awards, most of which were for swimming. Swimming he believed was a Christian duty. If preaching saved souls, swimming saved lives; it behoved every decent English Christian to master at least the breast-stroke. He sponsored numerous proficiency awards and introduced a national scheme – surely much abused – whereby every boy who taught another to swim received two shillings. Membership of the Canoe Club (the Commodore was HRH The Prince of Wales but the Captain and founder was John MacGregor, Esq.) was actually withheld from any non-swimmers; it was written in the rules.

In the perfect world everyone would swim and there would be no one to save. The Christian ideal should aim at a self-reliant amphibiousness for all mankind. When, in his early twenties, a friend had introduced him to the possibility of a portable boat it was as if he had been vouchsafed a glimpse of the City of God. Here was the perfect solution, an amphibious conversion kit. For what he had in fact been shown was not a boat at all but a coat or cloak. It was made of india-rubber and for added warmth in the winter it could be inflated. What could be inflated, reasoned MacGregor, could also float. It could be employed as a tent, as a bed (in essence it was of course a wraparound air-bed) and, most important of all, as a boat. 'Perhaps I shall go to the Lakes next year,' he mused in his diary.

This was in May 1848; by then MacGregor was studying for the Bar. He had come down from Cambridge with a degree in mathematics and an abiding interest in engineering, especially marine engineering. He had also formed his religious ideas, prayer meetings having featured as prominently in his syllabus as rowing and boxing.

In London the Temple became his home and patent law his profession; he was called to the Bar in 1851. But the Law could neither absorb his energy nor assuage his sense of mission. Of considerable private means, he did not need to practise. Instead he involved himself in a bewildering variety of philanthropic causes and went in for challenging holidays.

In 1849 he toured the Mediterranean and the Middle East. He shot a crocodile on the Nile, timed a tortoise across the field of Marathon, and compiled a much admired work on Arab music. The year 1852 found him in Ireland researching the openings for Protestant evangelists and in 1853, while making a Grand Tour of the Continent, he climbed Mont Blanc with a party of like-minded Englishmen which included William Russell of *The Times*. Only MacGregor and one other made it to the top. 'We were nos. 33 and 34 of those who have ascended Mont Blanc; . . . drank a bottle of champagne there and had breakfast.' Six weeks later he was boiling his breakfast eggs in the crater of Vesuvius.

Lapland was his next destination and, in 1857, Spain, ostensibly to investigate the claim of a Spaniard to have invented the steamship. In 1858 he went amongst 'our brothers and cousins in North America' ('the American citizen is our cousin by nationality but the American Christian is our brother at once and forever'). It was not the most enjoyable of his tours and what with slavery and bad table manners he found much to deplore. But it served one useful purpose: the Indian canoes on Lake Ontario immediately put him in mind of that inflatable coat. True, the canoe was unwearable; but you could sleep in it or under it, pull it anywhere and paddle it anywhere. And as a boat it was infinitely more stable, racy and respectable than the inflatable. He resolved to investigate further.

Once again other commitments intervened. He made a tour of Sweden and Russia, as far as Nijni Novgorod, and another of the Eastern Mediterranean and North Africa; it was here that he mastered the riding techniques of the 'Bedouin desert ranger'. At home he took up part-time soldiering. He organised and commanded the only company of London Volunteers to wear the kilt and on three successive years he carried off the shield for the best marksman. It was not till 1865 that the canoe at last found its way to the top of his pile of schemes pending. 'Idea about canoe voyage was in germ today', he wrote in his diary under May 28. Ten days later came 'Canoe project hatched', and on June 27, 'Saw *Rob Roy* completed'. Never one to detain a bee in his bonnet, on July 9 he shoved off from the Embankment just above the Houses of Parliament, shot under Westminster Bridge, narrowly missed the piers of Blackfriars Bridge, and made Gravesend by nightfall. Flushed with success he stocked up on chocolate and pushed off on the next morning's tide. The possibilities of his novel craft were almost too delicious to contemplate. Vistas of inexhaustible delight beckoned from every muddy ditch and sedgy mere. Lighting a cigar he set his sail and lolled back dreaming of fjords and canals, mighty rivers and mountain torrents. He could go anywhere; the world was at the tip of his paddle.

In walking you are bounded by every sea and river, and in a common sailing boat you are bounded by every shallow and shore; whereas I was in a canoe, which could be paddled or sailed, hauled or carried, over land or water to Rome, if I liked, or to Hong Kong.

Southend was as far as he got that night. A certain caution became necessary when a school of porpoises tried to adopt him, and off Shoeburyness he was finally defeated by heavy rain and a boisterous gale. But the *Rob Roy* had behaved beautifully. He immediately bought tickets for Dover by train, Ostend by the ferry, and Namur by train again. Within a week he was dipping his paddle in the Meuse.

The four months that followed were sheer delight. 'I never enjoyed so much continuous pleasure.' He explored the Meuse, Rhine, Main, Danube, Reuss, Aar, Ill, Moselle, Marne and Seine as well as lakes Titisee, Untersee, Constance, Zurich and Lucerne plus a few nameless canals. In the process he discovered that the canoeist has more fun paddling downstream than up and that the lower, navigable reaches of rivers are less exciting than their humbler upper reaches. Much of the time was consequently spent in Southern Germany and Switzerland and much of the itinerary consisted of portage. Fortunately he had had the first *Rob Roy* made of manageable proportions. Although built of oak with cedar decking, it weighed only eighty pounds. He could drag it himself, and with one volunteer could easily manhandle it into the lofts, barns and parlours where it was usually billeted for the night. The length was fifteen feet – 'just short enough to go into the German railway waggons' – and it drew a mere three inches of water; he could float it in a generous puddle.

Canoeing entailed a close acquaintance with water. 'For days together I had my feet bare and my trousers tucked up ready to wade at any moment.' Slithering down rapids, ploughing across reedy marshes, shying round bathing cattle, and plunging over small waterfalls, he guddled his way between, and usually slightly below, adjacent meadows. Worse in the catalogue of hazards were weirs, overhanging branches, and the wires used for pulling small country ferries across the stream. 'I never had a positive upset but of course I had to jump out frequently to save the boat.' It was all part of the canoeist's apprenticeship and he loved every minute of it. He loved the set pieces, as when a whole town turned out to watch the *Rob Roy* being put through her paces, or when some fancied danger lived up to expectations. And he loved the pastoral interludes that left him free to marvel at the ways of herons and moorhens, or to take by surprise the hay-making labourers and the riverside washerwomen.

It was one of those long cloudless summers; Europe was at peace, the harvest was bountiful, and the vintage promising. Being English and a canoeist, and being uncommonly proud of both, MacGregor observed with a quizzical detachment. But except for the customs officers of the Grand Duchy of Baden, whose insistence on examining the *Rob Roy*'s effects was an affront tantamount to making a body search of her skipper, and except for popery, which he could never under any circumstances condone, he extended a genial indulgence to all that was foreign. His notebooks and sketch-pads filled with anecdotes in which the laugh was as often on the author as on the onlooker.

Back in London for the winter, his new-found enthusiasm could not be contained. He wrote a bestselling book, *A Thousand Miles in the Rob Roy Canoe*, founded the Canoe Club, 'for business and bivouac, for paddling and sailing, and for racing and chasing in canoes over land and water', designed a new canoe, the *Rob Roy II*, and planned his next jaunt. The new boat was more lavishly equipped; it included 'the galley' (i.e. the bag with the spirit stove, eggs and spoon-cum-fork). And like the new expedition itself, it was shorter and faster. For three weeks he would paddle through the 'entanglement of water in rivers, lakes and pools' between Christiania, Stockholm and Gothenburg, then cross the Skagerrak for a few days coasting the Danish islands and the estuaries of the Elbe and Weser. Instead of portage by rail and cart he took to hailing passing steamers and thus hitch-hiking from one paddle to the next. If the people were less amusing, they were no less amused. The resultant book, *The Rob Roy in the Baltic*, was another resounding success.

Critics found it hard to censure such harmless enthusiasm. One ventured that 'mortals of less buoyant spirits might get tired of sitting in a damp tub, paddling in a confined attitude, and being restricted to watercourses as the only available routes'. Another felt bound to protest over the upstart canoe being projected as a pleasure craft; such it could never be 'when its only method of propulsion is based on the most wasteful expenditure of man's powers ever invented'. But, for MacGregor himself they had nothing but bemused admiration. He was described as an aquatic centaur, 'his lower part being a boat and his upper a wandering Englishman'; would he not be more comfortable with his legs amputated, it was asked. He had afforded the European nations 'strong confirmation of the eccentricity, not to say madness, of Britons' but he had also set a fine example of perseverance against all odds.

The traditional John Bull would have been shot at, arrested, stoned, cut down by scythes, or burnt as a wizard before he had accomplished the smallest part of Mr MacGregor's journey. He would have quarreled with the railway officials for refusing to take his canoe in the luggage van. When asked on a French canal to show his pass he would have knocked down the querist. He would certainly not have received the curiosity of whole towns as a compliment, or have delayed his start to accommodate a bedridden old man who particularly wished to see it. He must have lost his temper at having to paddle through a forest of grass four feet high, and would probably have remained there to this day. For a canoe voyage has its drawbacks, and paddling through a jungle is one of them. When Mr MacGregor gets soused in a rapid or tumbles sideways over a weir, he does not mind because it is all in the day's work.

In spite of such warnings canoe-mania soon raged. MacGregor, although he had neither invented the canoe nor introduced it, epitomised the craze. He was simply 'MacGregor the Canoe Man'. When Napoleon III, himself a *Rob Roy* fan, sanctioned a regatta in Paris in 1867 it was MacGregor and the Prince of Wales who planned the British participation and it was the two *Rob Roy* canoes that attracted the biggest crowds. MacGregor arrived in the Seine by yacht, or rather yawl. It was another one-man craft but far more commodious than a canoe, having hold-space for several hundredweight of tracts. These were duly distributed amongst the regatta-going public.

At this point in his canoeing career MacGregor could reasonably have stepped down. He was forty-three, heavily committed to other, and worthier, causes, and already assured of posterity's cognisance as 'the patron saint of canoeing'. It was time to ship his paddle – or at least to confine himself to home waters with perhaps the occasional dash through the breakers to some forlorn lighthouse. And had canoeing been to him just a gimmick or a sport, that is surely what he would have done. But it was, of course, very much more. It was a way of publicising his philanthropic activities and one which was already paying handsome dividends in royalties, press attention and popular support. More important, it was still, to MacGregor, a symbol and an example of the Christian mission. The canoe that could go anywhere was the perfect vessel for the evangelist. It knew no barriers and it

22

probed deep into the human heartland. It epitomised the individual's responsibility to chart his own course to salvation and it afforded a practical demonstration of that amphibious buoyancy which would enable the soul to ride out the storm and seek safe haven. This marvellous creation he had yet to display in a setting or on a mission appropriate to its deeper significance: hence, in 1868, the idea of his greatest and his most bizarre journey. He would take the *Rob Roy* to the Holy Land.

The *Rob Roy* was in fact *Rob Roy III*, and since this was the year before the Suez Canal was due to be opened, he decided to include Egypt: the idea was to ensure that the first boat through the canal should be the canoe. Then he would head for Palestine, explore and navigate the entire course of the Jordan river, and in the process identify the sites of biblical history. The canoe and its evangelical skipper would thus make an original contribution to Bible studies. Nothing could be more appropriate.

First, though, Egypt. The *Rob Roy* was launched from the *Tanjore* as soon as she dropped anchor in Alexandria harbour.

Her polished cedar deck glistened in the African sun and the waves of a new sea played along her smooth oak sides. The dockyard workmen ran to see the canoe, shouting in their scant attire. The sailors of a hundred vessels peered over their bulwarks to gaze at her dark blue sails and gilded silken flag; even the lonely sentry on the wall was aroused by the sight of the little English *merkeb* that skimmed over the sea so near to the breakers.

He quickly moved on to Port Said and the entrance to the canal. 'Collars and razors retire today into private life,' he wrote in his first letter to the Canoe Club. He was making 'decided progress in Arabic' – a progress that seems to have been speedily arrested – and was learning the Gospel by heart. A copy of *The Times*, without which no *Rob Roy* voyage would have been complete, he planned to 'use by bits up to Suez'. And although it was a torrid October his old grey flannel suit (grey because this was infidel and therefore enemy territory) was 'just the thing for this'.

He put up at the Hotel de France and paddled out through the flamingoes and pelicans of Lake Menzaleh to test for leaks.

In the shallows he was immediately surrounded by a mob of screaming Arab children.

Their frolics were very forward to say the least but boys, black or white, must be humoured to be ruled. So I appointed the noisiest of them as policeman and paid him a month's salary in advance – one penny – for which he made the rest drag the canoe with me in it a long way cheerfully. At last I got out of the boat and, wading in the soft mud, spoiled forever a pair of chamois shoes, twenty years old but never meant for use in water like this. 'Bakshish' was thus the first cry I heard in the East and the last I heard there after wandering long was 'Bakshish'.

Although a seasoned traveller, MacGregor had at first mis-heard this familiar greeting. Outside the hotel he had thought the little urchins were yelling not 'Bakshish, sir, bakshish' but 'Black shoes, sir, black shoes'. He had stopped in his tracks. This familiar London street call was music to his ear; for amongst his various home-based enterprises none had been more successful than his work as founder and chairman of the Shoeblack Brigade.

He had espoused the cause of slum children soon after coming down from Cambridge. As a leading light in the Ragged Schools Union, he had taught in their makeshift schools, withstood the usual barrage of rotten fruit and abuse, and busily organised funds and sponsors for what would one day become the work of the welfare state. But educating the underprivileged was only half the battle; to woo the waifs and the strays away from petty crime and remorseless penury what was needed was some sort of youth employment scheme. In 1851 the expected influx of visitors for the Great Exhibition had suggested a solution. He launched the Ragged Schools Shoeblack Society, soon to become the Shoeblack Brigade.

Ten shillings per boy begged or borrowed from a host of friends and patrons covered the initial outlay on box, brushes, polish and a dazzling scarlet uniform. In an alley off the Strand the new recruits were taught their trade 'chiefly on the feet of the committee who ran out now and then to get a splash of mud in the street puddles'. At last two star pupils were deployed, one outside the National Gallery and the other in Leicester Square. Crowds gathered, the boys took unkindly to some disparaging remarks about their uniforms, and the police were called in. But by the time the Exhibition opened the novelty was wearing off. The police had been mollified and there was a red-coated shoeblack on every street corner. The idea quickly spread to every borough in the capital and every city in the realm. Tens of thousands of boys participated and by the end of the century the Brigade's turnover would soar to £100,000 per annum. MacGregor remained 'the life and soul of the movement'. According to a contemporary 'it was his hobby, his pet idea; he loved it and he loved every member of the Brigade, rough, uncouth and almost brutal as some of them were in their original state'.

When not abroad with the *Rob Roy* he never missed the seven a.m. assembly of shoeblacks at their Strand head-quarters. He conducted the morning service, which like the evening lessons was all part of the Brigade's rehabilitating programme, and then despatched each boy to his station with a word of encouragement.

Nor was this the only venture of its kind to spring from MacGregor's fertile brain. There were also the 'broomers' who swept the pavement in front of your shop every morning for sixpence a week. And the 'steppers' – 'little girls in neat frocks and straw bonnets' who washed your doorstep and whitened it with pipeclay. There was a corps of window-cleaners, another of newspaper boys, and another of messengers. And given a few more days in Port Said there would no doubt have been a corps of small boys for pulling small boats.

In the absence of any such organisation a tall Nubian helped him launch the *Rob Roy* on the canal itself. The wind was from the north and the canal dead straight for thirty miles. He set his sails and fell to contemplating the work of 'making Africa into an island'. Steam dredges and cranes, fuelled by convoys of coal barges, clanked and rattled as they scoured out the sand and dumped it alongside in high banks. MacGregor conjectured that it would all be blown back and that the canal would never pay. But he admired the daring and the industry.

Soon after sunset he moored near Ras el Esh, boiled a cube

of Liebig's soup, and prepared to turn in. Just as the *Rob Roy II*
had seen the introduction of the galley, so the *Rob Roy III* saw
the introduction of the Captain's cabin.

This canoe was built round me reclining as my first one had been built
round me sitting – in each case recognising the one great principle, far too
often neglected, that a comfortable boat, like a shoe or a coat, must be *made*
for the wearer and not *worn down* to his shape.

In preparing for the night the first thing was to work the boat
well into the sand. Then, by removing a small section of deck
and using the paddle as a roof tree, a large sheet of oilskin was
draped over to make the whole into a tent and the hull into a
bed. Inside this went a mosquito-net and his air mattress, the
latter being a stingy three feet by fourteen inches – 'quite long
enough', though; 'it is only the shoulders and hips that really
require a soft mattress; as for the rest of one's body it doesn't
matter at all' – except that the head needed a pillow, to which
end he fluffed up the post-office bag in which his dry clothes
were stored.

At Ras el Esh, in spite of these comforts, he slept badly; the
spot in which he had bedded the canoe was evidently a desert
latrine. Next night his visitors were not insects but dogs, large,
bristling, jackal-like creatures with erect tails and much
effrontery. He reached for his pistol but somehow they knew
just when to slink off.

Kantara followed and here he rested. It was Sunday; he
always rested on Sundays. But the cranes and dredges did not;
and, by way of divine displeasure, a sandstorm engulfed the
place. The particles were so fine that they even penetrated his
mosquito-net. He spent another restless night by the canal
and at last paddled into Ismailia.

Ismailia is the half-way point on the Suez Canal, but in
1868 it was as far as the canal went; the next section was still
being excavated. MacGregor knew this; he also knew of the
Sweetwater Canal, an older construction that ran parallel to
the line of the new canal from Ismailia to Suez on the Red Sea.
Although transferring from one waterway to another might be
out of the question for most of the world's shipping, it was just
what the canoe was for. On a few yards of desert portage

would rest his claim to have sailed the first vessel from the Mediterranean to the Red Sea without going round the Cape.

At this point he was joined by Michael Hany, dragoman to the Prince of Wales, who had masterminded his previous tours in the Middle East and who now again entered Mac-Gregor's employ. 'A really excellent fellow', Hany quickly persuaded his employer that in the absence of a second canoe he should hire a local boat to carry luggage, afford protection and generally act as mother-ship. Thus, in convoy, they paddled and sailed south. At dinner time, under the new arrangement, a table was erected across the gunwales of the larger boat and one of Hany's underlings acted as waiter 'handing up the dishes as he stood impassive in the cold water'.

The Sweetwater Canal skirted the Bitter Lakes and then dropped through locks towards Suez. MacGregor had now finished his only copy of *The Times* and was struggling with a French translation of Speke's journey to the source of the Nile. He had picked it up in Ismailia and, as always, ripped off its covers before starting. In a canoe every ounce counted. Now he tore out each page as he read it.

Once, in the midday, a man shouted at me to approach the bank for he had a letter for me. After reading the letter I put it in my breast-pocket, when at the same moment a beautiful little fish leapt from the water into my pocket with the letter. The bystanders shouted eagerly at this undoubted sign of good luck; and I had the fish broiled for dinner, occupying the centre of a large flat dish. The extreme length of the fish was under two inches but the happy omen from it lasted for months.

The Bitter Lakes had evidently once been part of the Red Sea. It must therefore have been in the vicinity of Suez that the waters parted for the passage of the Israelites. MacGregor found a likely ridge that once might have been the very ford and then paddled off down the Red Sea coast to Ain Musa, the Well of Moses. Originally the plan had been to canoe right round the Sinai peninsula to Aqaba, but Hany was against this and, after a look at the forbidding coastline, so was MacGregor. Instead they would head back to Port Said along the Nile and then take ship to Beirut.

Before leaving Suez he treated his fellow guests at the local hotel to a lecture on canoeing. Amongst them was a forceful young man who afterwards collared MacGregor and introduced himself as 'Mr Stanley of the *New York Herald Tribune*'. He expressed great interest in the *Rob Roy* and borrowed a copy of MacGregor's first book. Next morning he announced that he had sat up all night reading it and that he was now going to telegraph a story which would alert all America to the *Rob Roy*'s doings. MacGregor was most grateful.

What a sensational set these Yankees are! In return I gave him a short letter of introduction to Dr Livingstone and he went off to meet him and to get the first news for America from Livingstone's lips as to whether he went round Lake Tangayika and so solved the problem of the Nile and its source.

MacGregor knew and admired David Livingstone. Indeed, had he not been so appalled by the misery to be found in London's slums, he would willingly have joined the Doctor in Africa. The two men had first met in Ireland in 1857 when MacGregor had been enlisted to promote a scheme for encouraging the Africans to grow cash crops and so reduce their dependence on slavery. But of Livingstone's whereabouts in 1868 he could presume no greater knowledge than Stanley.

He had also drawn the illustrations for Livingstone's *Missionary Travels and Researches in South Africa*. As an artist MacGregor produced effective and usually faithful delineations of buildings and vegetation. Less true to life were his people. He was much influenced by *Punch*, to which he often contributed, and by the idea that the artist's job was to entertain. If this meant giving everyone funny faces and baggy clothes, then so be it. To MacGregor as a writer the same criticism applies. As in his lectures, he set out to win laughs. Often his published narrative was at variance with the record of events as related in his letters. He rearranged, coloured and distorted freely. Since his contributions to scholarship were usually incidental he saw no reason to shackle his narrative with the ponderous weight of academic scruple. To sell books and so publicise worthy causes, raise money and win converts for the canoe, it was essential never to be dull.

But such deliberate humour would soon have palled without his genius for observation. After dutifully recommending Cairo's one and only Ragged School to the generosity of his readers, he paddled off into the Nile delta. Threading a maze of sluggish arteries, he rejoiced as the lush scenery closed in around him. After the barren sands of Sinai he was back in a familiar paradise of grassy meadows and tall trees alive with sparrows. There were ducks to be shot and fish to be hooked. Here was a village of dovecotes; amongst the reeds butterflies basked 'as if poised on sunbeams'; and here piped the king-fisher, his particular favourite.

When I desired to watch these birds, the halcyons of antiquity, I quietly moved my boat until it grounded, and after it was stationary for a few moments the Halcyon fisher got quite unconcerned and plied his task as if unseen. He peers with knowing eye into the shallow below him and now and then dips his head to make quite sure he has marked a fish worth seizing. Then suddenly he darts down with a flash and flies off with a little white minnow or a struggling stickleback nipped in his beak. If it is caught crosswise the winged fisherman tosses his prey in the air and nimbly catches it so that it may be gulped down properly. Then he quivers and shakes with satisfaction and quickly speeds to another perch, flitting by you with wonderful swiftness, as if a sapphire had been flung athwart a sunbeam, flashing beauteous colours in its flight. Or if bed time has come and he is fetching home the Sunday dinner, he flutters on and on and then with a sharp note of good-bye, pops into a hole, the dark staircase to his tiny nest. There he finds Mrs Halcyon sitting in state, and thirteen baby kingfishers gaping for the dainty dish.

On Lake Menzaleh, which he now re-entered, the flocks of ducks, geese, swans and flamingoes formed compact masses, like islands, which rose when he paddled near and whirred overhead in dazzling clouds. Such a heaven-sent conjunction of distinguished marksman and quacking, honking plenty was almost an embarrassment. 'Tender qualms about gay feathers fluttering at end of my gun-barrel and unconsciously awaiting their doom' stayed his trigger finger. He actually longed to miss. 'For 'tis better to grumble at one's bad luck or bad shooting than to be haunted by the ghosts of orphan ducklings or the cackling of a web-footed widow.'

But the pelicans he could not resist. They rode the water like battleships. Stuffed, what a talking piece, what a worthy addition to his lecture props. On his last day in Africa he paddled out from Port Said bent on slaughter. There were those who averred that the kick from a 12-bore fired broadside would surely capsize the canoe. But MacGregor was more worried about his gun. Like that spoon-cum-fork, this all-purpose weapon was another product of his weight-conscious ingenuity; it was double-barrelled but one barrel was rifled for ball and the other smooth for shot. Unfortunately this innovation seemed to have impaired the accuracy of both barrels. It was, he decided, the only possible explanation. After much manoeuvring and a long wait for the moment when both canoe and pelican rose simultaneously on the crest of a wave, he fired, and he missed, 'and that was an end to it'. Next day he sailed for Beirut and phase two of the journey.

Although the Lebanon had rivers, none of them was of much scriptural interest. While MacGregor toured Beirut distributing tracts and calling on the British and American missionaries, Hany arranged horses and a cart to transport the party across the mountains to Syria. By now it was early December. The road was deep in mud and on the pass above Zahleh they were overtaken by a blizzard. Still smarting from his failure with the pelicans, MacGregor sought revenge by shooting at a jackal, which he again missed, and at an eagle that was devouring a hare. He hit the hare. 'If my paddle had not been better than my powder, the *Rob Roy*'s cruise would have been rather a bore.' But, as he now admitted, it was one thing to pierce the bull on a rifle range, another to take on 'rough game' in the wild.

Tamer game awaited them at their first night stop in Syria. The house was infested with cats. MacGregor repulsed them with nuts, stones, his boots, and his paddle. They kept on coming. It made him long for that other Rob Roy, his dog, who had been left behind in London. Next morning work began in earnest.

Before tackling the Jordan he had resolved to sort out two short, insignificant, and extremely confusing rivers in the vicinity of Damascus. Called the Abana and the Pharpar, many maps in fact showed them as a single stream. No one knew which were their main sources, nor exactly where they ended. Probably no one much cared. But MacGregor, now steeped in the mystery of the Nile and the stirring tale of Burton and Speke, was determined to worry some sense out of their brief wanderings and so make his modest contribution to geographical science.

The Abana took precedence. He spent two days making a reconnaissance of the springs and rills that fed it before finally launching the *Rob Roy* at a point where it ran fast and furious between rocky crags and was 'about the size of a Scotch salmon stream'. After the smooth waters of the Suez Canal and the 'oily-running' Nile, here was a worthy challenge. Careering along at a river's gallop between rocks and forest, he again experienced that tickle in the midriff 'so often felt on a high rope swing'. No time here for bird-watching. A wrong choice at the first division of the stream found him drifting into a dark tunnel. The river went underground. Evidently its flow was much tapped for irrigation. (It was; the conduits and aqueducts which sustained cultivation around Damascus were the wonder of the Islamic world.) As a result the Abana was one of those rivers whose volume of water decreased the further it went. He hauled and waded back upstream and started again. This time he selected a stream which quickly whirled him into a deep twilight gorge choked by fallen trees. It was hard work forcing a way through these obstructions and Hany, watching his progress on the heights above, was out of earshot. At last the cliffs fell away and he was out in the sunshine again. The stream composed itself into a placid river and dead ahead rose the white walls and minarets of Damascus, 'the oldest city in the world'. A large crowd with a sumptuous picnic waited to receive him. There was something distinctly biblical about the procession which then bore the *Rob Roy* shoulder-high into the city and lowered her into a marble bath in the ornamental courtyard of Demetri's Hotel. Lying, as it were, in state, the Damascenes filed past her to pay their respects and satisfy their curiosity. MacGregor retired for a bath.

Twenty miles east of the city and on the edge of the desert, the Abana supposedly ended in the Lake, or swamp, of Ateibeh. To investigate this phenomenon, MacGregor and his men, now augmented by two Turkish soldiers – a concerned but totally useless present from the city's governor – rode forth on Christmas Eve. A tiring day was spent manhandling mules and canoe across a water-logged plain not unlike an Irish bog. At last they struck firm ground and made camp. 'The Red Ensign of England was soon hoisted on a tall pole to wave over as wild a spot as ever was seen.' Hard by, the Abana river, now just four yards wide, slid silently into a vast forest of reeds. This was the 'lake' and any normal explorer would have been happy to record its position and beat a hasty retreat.

But MacGregor wanted to make sure – or, if he were absolutely candid, to find some justification for having dragged the canoe to this God-forsaken spot. What he called 'quagmire navigation' could be both interesting and dangerous. The only other boat, 'a poor tub' by all accounts, ever to have essayed the swamp had been lost with all hands. Mud, through which you could neither swim nor wade, was more treacherous than water, and the place had an evil reputation for leopards, wild boar, and lethal miasmas..

'Still, the thing must be done somehow.' To trace a runnel of water until it flowed no further was the object, and never was a matter of so little import accorded such careful planning. Compass bearings were taken, signals pre-arranged, the boat provisioned, the gun loaded, and prayers said. Having tied his solar topi with a silk scarf on which was emblazoned the badge of the Canoe Club, the grey-flannelled explorer poled, paddled and punted off into the unknown.

The forest of reeds closed behind him. Taking the first of several pre-cut strips of calico he tied it to a tall clump of canes and recorded its position in his log book. 'From this, called Station No 1, I worked on until it was nearly invisible and then tied Station No 2, and so on.' The plan worked admirably.

At length I reached a point where all stream ceased as was shown when the mud stirred by my pole did not advance beyond my boat at rest – in fact the *Rob Roy* was now in the middle of the marsh.

'Four hours of tremendous labour' had earnt him a good lunch. With flannels steaming he tucked into the pick of his

4 'Handing up the dishes as he stood impassive in the cold water'.
The *Rob Roy* is moored alongside the mother ship as MacGregor dines
on the Sweetwater Canal
5 'It was a crisis now'. Prize taking on the river Jordan

The original sketch for the first.
Circular of the Ragged school Shoeblack Society
A.D. 1851

6 1851, The Great Exhibition, and MacGregor's Shoeshine Brigade
goes into action

provisions and marvelled at the still silence of his position. On the summit of Mont Blanc or at the bottom of a Swedish coal mine he had never felt more removed from the world. But for all the elaborate preparations and the extravagant sentiments, nothing can disguise the fact that MacGregor's exploration of Lake Ateibeh ranks as one of the great non-events of nineteenth-century endeavour. Instead of rampaging boar and aquatic leopards, his only visitation was from a single bewildered mosquito. 'He did not bite; perhaps he had never been taught that man is the sweetest morsel.' Few explorers would come so near to unintentionally parodying their genre.

Back in camp his safe return was celebrated with roast turkey. It was, after all, Christmas Day. A bonfire was lit and after the plum pudding MacGregor emerged from his tent to address the company.

The moon shone clear and our fire had become embers when the *Howaja* [i.e. MacGregor himself] joined the party round it and asked silence. He told them that we had now reached the furthest point of our journey. After this we were going south and west and homewards. Then he turned to the journey of life, and the home for us pilgrims, then to Christmas Day just finished as a great mark in time's road to eternity, and then he gave them a condensed history of the world from the creation – the law – the prophets and the Saviour – the apostles – the martyrs and ourselves.

Hany translated into Arabic and 'every sentence was heard with intense interest'. Long after lights-out the men were still discussing its import. 'Perhaps no one of them had ever heard so much truth before, or would ever hear it again.' To this open-air sermon the time and place could hardly have lent greater poignancy. On the distant hills shepherds were out watching their flocks; there was a star in the East – in fact several; and if there was no baby there was at least the *Rob Roy*, lashed in the cradle by which it was carried on horseback. 'By now even the men loved her.'

When it came to 'open-air sermons' MacGregor knew all the tricks in the book. Along with shoeblacks, canoes, and schools for the poor, preaching was one of his pet hobbyhorses. While pacing London's pavements in the early days of the Shoeblack Brigade he had become alarmed at the number

33

of street corner fanatics promulgating fringe beliefs and heresies. There were Mormons, Free-thinkers, Communists, rabid Teetotallers, Spiritualists and, above all and most insidious of all, Papists. But where was the voice of sound, commonsensical, English religion? Clearly it was time someone spoke out for the 'good old Gospel'. As heckler, protagonist, and then orator, MacGregor had progressed to his own soap-box and cast about for allies.

In 1853, with two other like-minded evangelists, he founded the Open-Air Mission, 'a small beginning of what may – yea, will be – a great, a noble, a blessed undertaking'. They drew a little map of London and put crosses at all those intersections and parks, from Tower Hill to Parliament Hill, where a preacher could hope to attract an audience. Soon the Mission was fielding fiery churchmen 'not afraid to bare their arms to save souls' at a dozen different locations. Each Sunday, like a captain doing the rounds of the watch, MacGregor paid them a visit.

June 24 1855. With Maunsell to Edward Street where I spoke to 20 men and women and they thanked us. Then to James Street. Found Shaw and Cozens and Fowell; Shaw spoke on 'the wages of sin' but not in simple language. I spoke to them afterwards of the Good Shepherd when they attended well. Went out to top of Edward Street and spoke to 100 on Sodom and Gomorrah. Some at distance threw mud, cabbage stalks, stones and oyster shells. Hit my hat several times, my cheek and coat and waistcoat covered. Still many heard well and thanked us ... Told to leave as a disturbance was threatened. To Hyde Park where open-air meeting about Sunday Question had been announced. Cozens preaching, standing on a seat under a tree. 200 heard; several interrupted, mostly Papists ... In all I attended eight open-air services today and thank God that much was heard and said to make men wise unto salvation.

His conviction was ever that what he called 'the good old Gospel' should be taken at its literal value. Suspicious of intellectual subtlety under any guise, he branded even churchmen, if they favoured a freer interpretation, as 'sceptics'. Every word in the Bible withstood honest scrutiny; he would challenge anyone to prove otherwise. And in 1868, as the *Rob Roy* at last drew nigh unto the Holy Land, he would miss no opportunity to hammer home this conviction.

To those who found the Old Testament's topography as

indigestible as its genealogies, his pronouncements must have meant little; here was the kingdom of Og and here the land of Bashan. Every pile of masonry seemed to bear on scriptural authenticity. After a long trek from the graveyard of the Abana to the nursery streams of the Jordan he identified the spring at Banias as the site of Caesarea Philippi, that at El Kadi as the city of Dan, and a snake-infested ruin on the river's third feeder as Hazor 'which shall be a dwelling place for dragons'. On all these pools and trickles the canoe was dutifully launched for a few token paddle strokes. Only one humble spring was without any association and was therefore christened Ain Rob Roy.

To MacGregor it was a matter of profound shame that the Jordan, sacred alike to Christian, Muslim and Jew, and therefore the most revered river in the world, should not be better charted. Not only was there uncertainty about its various sources but, for a short section through the marshes of Lake Hooleh, even its course was untraced.

Suppose we had ten miles of the Thames still uncertain on our maps, would it not be a reproach to English boatmen? But Jordan was an old river before the Thames was heard of and the Thames will be forgotten when the Jordan will be remembered forever. What an honour then for the *Rob Roy* to trace even one new bend of this ancient river!

There were, as he was about to discover, reasons for this apparent neglect. Lake Hooleh was going to test to the utmost his vaunted skills in 'quagmire navigation'; and the marsh Arabs who inhabited its malarial flats would more than justify their unsavoury reputation. Had the Old Testament been a little more specific about this short section of the Jordan he might well have backed off.

His first mistake was to despatch Hany and his retinue before the *Rob Roy* was safely into the lake and before he had any idea whether it was possible to reach the pre-arranged rendezvous. The river itself looked promising enough. It was forty feet wide and fast-flowing between low grassy banks. Past the first village – a collection of wattle huts and a clump of palm trees – he slipped unnoticed. Then the current slowed and the line of the river buckled. He developed a new technique for negotiating the Z bends which involved ramming the bank, letting the canoe pivot, then back-paddling till the stern rammed the bank lower down, and so pivoting back to go full ahead out of the second bend. 'This new *pas* I called "waltzing", the *Rob Roy* being my fair partner.' It was such fun that the next village took him unawares. Suddenly the bank was alive with wild, gesticulating figures. Something about their manner set them apart from the normal run of spectators. They raced along beside him and they brandished clubs, sticks and spears.

In a bid to outdistance them he dug on the paddle and shot ahead. But the river continued to loop and his pursuers had thus merely to cut across the corners. Stones and mud-balls splattered around him. The pack was now a hundred strong; some stripped off their clothes as they ran and at the third bend they were strung across the river waiting for him. 'It was a crisis now.' A black arm hooked around the stern of the boat but was levered off with a flick of the paddle. He thought he was safe, then he noticed a man on the bank who was crouching very still and had a gun in his shoulder.

He was cool, and so was I. The muzzle was not twenty feet from my face. Three thoughts coursed through my brain: 'Will hit me in the mouth; bad to lie wounded here.' 'Aims from his left shoulder; how convenient to shoot from both sides.' 'No use bobbing here; first time under fire; Arabs respect courage.' The clear round black of the muzzle end followed me covering as I passed. I stared right at the man's eyes and gave one powerful stroke; at the same moment he fired – fizz, bang! and a splash of the bullet in the water behind me. Loud shouts came out of the smoke. I stopped and said, 'Not fair to use gun!' In an instant the water was full of naked swimmers.

One grabbed the stern, another who was brandishing a gigantic bone secured the bow. 'His face was black, his cheeks were deeply gashed and tattooed, he had one big ear-ring, his top-knot stood erect, and the water glistened on his huge naked carcase as he roughly grasped my delicate little paddle.' MacGregor's pistol was between his legs, but he hesitated to use it. Instead he opted for a policy of injured but genial innocence. Ignoring the screams for bakshish he politely thanked his captors for their pressing invitation to land and begged silence for a short announcement. 'Ingleez,' he explained, 'Ingleez.'

They replied 'Sowa, sowa' (friends) and then rubbed their two forefingers together, the usual sign of amity. I said it was not fair to use the 'baroda' (gun). Holding up one finger I said 'Ingleez wahed' (one Englishman), then holding up both hands I said 'Araby kooloo' (all the rest Arabs). At this the crowd applauded, laughing, and so did I.

Regrettably a little girl chose this moment to discharge a sod of earth onto the *Rob Roy*. MacGregor slowly inspected the horrid mess and then turned to her elders with a look of bewildered entreaty. 'It was a turning point this.' They were evidently uneasy; some actually chose to chastise the small girl. Meanwhile, how to conceal his pistol? Already hands were probing under the waterproof apron. If he got out they would surely discover it. Yet they would scarcely release him without demanding an inspection.

Suddenly the *Rob Roy* gave an unfamiliar lurch and began to rise out of the water. The boat was being impounded with her captain still aboard. Hoisted to shoulder height she was swaying up the bank and into the village.

The men were rough and boisterous. The boat heeled and plunged as if in a terrible sea. I clasped the two nearest bearers round their necks to steady these surgings.

He was deposited in the tent of the village sheikh and there at last extricated himself from both boat and pistol. The crowd was ordered back while he made a leisurely inspection of his new surroundings. 'The first thing to recollect in this sort of adventure is that time is of no consequence to such people but that stage effect and dignity are very important to your case.'

Feeling altogether more confident, he vigorously shook the sheikh's hand and thanked him for the use of his tent as a rest camp. 'I saw he was a second rate man without much decision in his mien.' Under cover of exhibiting the 'galley', 'cabin' etc. he slipped him a gold napoleon. 'He whispered "Shwei, shwei" (softly, quietly) and I knew I had bought him then.' To drive home his advantage MacGregor now primed his stove and set about producing beef broth, thereby exposing his host's failure to have yet come up with an offer of refreshment. The broth needed salt. He dug out the snuff-box that served as a salt-cellar and offered some to the sheikh. Thinking it was sugar, the poor man took a generous pinch.

Instantly I ate up the rest of the salt and with a loud laughing shout, I administered to the astonished and outwitted sheikh a manifest thump on the back . . . We had now eaten salt together, and in his own tent, and so he was bound by the strongest tie, and he knew it.

While the assembled company debated his case MacGregor enjoyed a substantial lunch and read *The Times*. Nothing in all his travels could compare with the present incident and he was now determined to milk it for all it was worth. Informed that he might leave the next day, he rose slowly, stood on tiptoe, raised an arm to the roof, and thundered, 'Tomorrow. No. English.' 'Then the orator sunk calmly down and went on reading his paper again.'

This extraordinary performance won the day. The Arabs were not just outmanoeuvred but overawed. However sizeable a ransome this long, grey-flannelled water sprite might command, they had no wish for any dealings with the brethren of such an unpredictable exotic. Without further ado the *Rob Roy* was returned to the river and escorted downstream.

But the river soon forked into thickets and swamp; evidently it was the beginning of the 'lake'. Here the thickets were even thicker and the patches of clear water even fewer than at Ateibeh. For perhaps a mile he shoved, hauled, and waded, then gave up. There was positively no way through – and given the ingredients of a lively narrative, there was every reason for turning back to the village of his erstwhile captors. There experiences new and amusing could be confidently expected.

Ideally a day of such high drama should end with reconciliation. When the Arabs invited him to join them for their dinner of kuskus and meat he therefore accepted willingly and contributed a whole rice pudding. After dinner they sat out late under the stars sharing a pipe. His neighbour was the man who had taken the pot-shot at him; but who could blame the poor fellow?

When they suddenly saw a thing with a man's face, but all the rest of it unlike a man – a long brown double-ended body joined by grey skin to a grey, pot-shaped head, and waving about two blue hands (the paddle blades) – which of them could refrain from taking a shot at such a creature? Would you or I, walking with a loaded gun and eager for an excuse to fire, if we saw for the first time a thing in the air unknown and yet plainly living, could we resist the desire to fire at it instantly? Not I certainly.

MacGregor was warming to the Arabs much as he had to the slum children of the Ragged Schools. They knew not what they did. Yet they had furnished him with an opportunity to display qualities of a high moral order. Meeting their aggression with unflinching courage, frustrating their cunning with inexhaustible humour, and accepting their final overtures with the best possible grace, he had been able to set a new and ostentatious standard in roving heroics. His portrait of the noble and magnanimous hero would become a stock figure in the pages of the *Boy's Own Paper*. It comes as no surprise to find MacGregor subsequently heading a movement for the provision of wholesome literature for the young and in fact helping to found that very paper.

Reunited with the faithful Hany he completed the exploration of Lake Hooleh and, after a rather messy tussle, at last secured a pelican. He kept just the head and feet. There was no one to help him preserve the trophy and even these extremities quickly turned into a green jelly.

Thence to Galilee, otherwise Lake Tiberias or Gennesaret, which was supposed to be both the climax and conclusion of the tour. For three weeks he paddled back and forth exploring its shoreline and, in so far as was possible, its bed. The beach of Bethsaida and, above all, the site of Capernaum were matters of controversy into which he joined with intense enthusiasm and to which he contributed useful observations. Faith, of course, transcended geography; Christianity was for all times and all places. Which precisely was the bit of water on which Christ walked, or where exactly He preached, or what sort of fishes composed the miraculous draught, were not fundamental concerns. But nothing brought home the literal truth of Scripture like the identification and authentication of these matters. Every ruin, every hill and beach, could provide ammunition for an open-air slanging match with the Hyde Park Papists.

Only in one respect was Galilee a disappointment: there was very little drama. As if to make good this deficiency, while returning north to Beirut, he launched the *Rob Roy* for a final paddle on the Kishon river near Haifa. He was richly rewarded. Whether it really was a crocodile that poked its snout out of the water while he was breakfasting aboard is open to doubt. None had ever been recorded in Palestine before; he saw it only for a second; and he saw only the tip of its nose. But he was positive. He had, after all, seen crocodiles before; the one which he shot in the Nile was mounted in his study; for twenty years he had faced it across his desk. He had found crocodile footprints in the mud nearby. And he had actually felt the brute.

Just as I began to lean over to take a sketch of the footprints, I felt something hard under the boat's bottom, which began behind me (so not floating with the stream) and it went bump, bump, all along, exactly under my seat.

Later he admitted that it was probably very small. But it was still a crocodile and therefore a worthy climax both to his journey and to his subsequent lectures.

Returning to England in April 1869 he began that lecturing marathon and resumed his work with the Open-Air Mission, the Ragged Schools and the Shoeblacks. His energy was unabated; it seemed that only age or illness could staunch it. But in 1873, aged forty-eight, he surprised even his closest friends by getting married. His diary, so long the confidante of all his hopes and schemes, slowly petered out.

Dec 1	Preparations for execution.	
Dec 2	ditto	ditto
Dec 3	ditto	ditto
Dec 4	Wedding Day!	

The marriage was blessed with children and it was marital bliss that finally seduced him from public service. The firebrand became a much loved but little noticed family man. By the time of his death, in 1891, he was almost forgotten. For a parade of his achievements his wedding was considerably more revealing than his funeral. On the former occasion a thousand people filled the church in Blackheath and crowds more waited outside. The guard of honour was provided by boys of the *Chichester* flanked by scarlet-uniformed Shoeblacks. Two crossed paddles held by members of the Canoe Club formed an archway. Representatives of the Ragged Schools mingled with 'bare arm' preachers from the Open-Air Mission and kilted cockneys from the London Volunteers. Tracts, one may assume, circulated freely.

CHAPTER TWO
LOVE VERSUS LOCOMOTION
Captain John Dundas Cochrane

If the darkest hour is just before dawn the coldest week must be just before spring; and spring comes late in Estonia. The year of 1820 being no exception, first light on April 28 found the townsfolk of Narva reluctant to stir. The previous day's rain had turned to flurries of snow which whirled about the town's old fortress and subsided onto the frozen river at its base. A few miles downstream the Gulf of Finland, at the north-eastern corner of the Baltic, was still a boundless sheet of ice, its islands pocking the surface like frosted molehills. Too late for sledges and too early for sailing boats, its coastline was deserted.

This was disappointing to one as nautically minded as the small and tired tramp who turned into Narva in search of breakfast. All night he had trudged along the Gulf's north-facing shore hoping for some distraction. Now, as he slowed his pace, the cold began to penetrate his ragged overcoat. Ignoring such sights as this his first Russian town might boast, he sought out the smoky fug of the post inn. There he ordered black bread and coffee as the damp steamed from his person. The same fare on the previous morning had set him back one silver rouble; that was very nearly an English shilling. Such wild extravagance was to be avoided. If the Russian Empire was so much more expensive than the Prussian, all would depend on its also being more hospitable.

He eyed the inn's other patrons with revived interest. They paid no heed. But as he rose to plead his poverty with the landlord, providence, in the shape of a prosperous and imposing merchant, intervened. The newcomer was every vagrant's idea of the perfect patron. He would pay for breakfast; he was offering his spare carriage all the way to St Petersburg; and he promised full board and lodging en route.

Rather surprisingly, the tramp hesitated. He had no wish to appear ungrateful but the offer did raise a question of principle. Lifts, he explained, ran foul of his philosophy. He preferred to walk, usually it was cheaper to walk, and often, as he had just proved by overhauling the Riga to St Petersburg stage coach, it was quicker. On the other hand, he was sorely tempted. There was much to be said for entering the Russian capital in style; it was only two days' journey; and the scenery promised little in the way of novelty. Indeed the greatest novelty he had so far encountered in wintry Estonia was this merchant. For the man spoke uncommonly good English; and he was black.

With no one to perform the necessary introductions both men withheld their identities. The tramp celebrated his good fortune by ordering a second breakfast, then a room, while his benefactor – 'my sable companion', he called him – disappeared on urgent business. The urgent business proved to be an assignation with the chambermaid. It was early the following morning before the two men met again, and they then immediately parted, each to a separate carriage. The offer had evidently been accepted. All day they raced along the featureless shores of the Gulf. When they stopped for the night the negro again disappeared in quest of a chambermaid while the tramp was more than content with his second night in a bed. Next day they would reach St Petersburg.

Over their last breakfast the negro asked his impoverished companion whether he possessed such a thing as a passport. He did. The document was produced and inspected. It identified the bearer as one John Dundas Cochrane, Captain, R N. The negro, visibly discomfited, stared hard at the tramp.

'Cochrane? Is you kin to Admiral Cochrane who was in de West Indies at de capture of de Danish islands in 1807?'

'Indeed. I am his nephew.'

'Is you den de son of Massa Cochrane-Johnstone?'

'Yes, I am.'

'You is den that lilly Massa Johnny I knew at de same time.'

It now turned out [wrote Cochrane] that this black gentleman with the two carriages and the four horses each had been my father's and my uncle's servant thirteen years before. Having talked over old matters he remarked that he could never have recognised me for the alteration that time had made in my features, observing that I seemed to have verified the West Indian proverb, 'like the black man's pig, very lilly but damn old'.

By now the horses were ready. Outside the thaw had begun. And in an Estonian inn the topsy-turvy world of the traveller had been set to rights; the tramp was revealed as an officer and a gentleman whilst his prosperous-looking companion was just the servant and plaything of some Russian prince. 'Fortune's frolic was now explained,' wrote Cochrane as, riding in the first carriage, he entered St Petersburg. His sable companion, now a mere attendant, delivered him to respectable lodgings and withdrew. Their paths never crossed again. Cochrane never even learnt the man's name.

Nor had he any wish for further reminders of his childhood. 'Fortune's frolics' he knew too well. Born into one of Scotland's most martial clans he had nursed expectations of life. Besides the uncle, three of his first cousins were, or were about to become admirals. And one, the chief of the 'Fighting Cochranes', was the legendary Lord Thomas Cochrane, tenth Earl of Dundonald. In 1820, as John Dundas tramped into Russia, Thomas rode the high seas in command of the Chilean navy. For Captain Marryat, G. A. Henty and C. S. Forrester, Admiral Thomas Cochrane set a standard of derring-do which no fiction could match; they would simply appropriate his history.

A Cochrane who was not a sailor was usually a soldier. In the family tree colonels and generals outnumbered even the captains and admirals. Together, at any given time during the eighteenth and nineteenth centuries, they mustered enough officers to staff the armed forces of a minor nation.

Yet for John Dundas high rank was never more than a remote possibility. For one thing he had the misfortune of being illegitimate. Nothing is known of his mother except that her timing was impeccable – she gave birth on St Valentine's Day, 1793 – and that she was not The Lady Georgiana Johnstone whom his father married in the same year. Four years later Colonel the Hon. Andrew James Cochrane (now Cochrane-Johnstone) relinquished his parliamentary seat and accepted the governorship of Dominica in the West Indies. There 'Massa Johnny' had grown up; and there his father had laid the foundations of a most unsavoury reputation. During five years of misrule he dealt in slaves, kept a harem, and provoked his troops to mutiny. He also developed a taste for embezzlement and it was on this last score that in 1803 he was recalled and court-martialled.

In the same year John Dundas, aged ten, was sent to sea. No doubt the two events were connected. He served as midshipman on his uncle's flagship. For a Cochrane it was as good a schooling as any; it was also pretty much like home with no less than four other Cochranes serving on the same ship. Nothing if not loyal to his clan, the uncle even found a congenial post for John Dundas's disgraced father: he became customs officer on the island of Tortola. There he was again arrested for fraud but broke parole and turned his energies to gun-running. The guns generally failed to materialise; all the running was done by Cochrane-Johnstone himself. Eventually it took him back to England.

His masterstroke came in 1814. On the night of February 20 the landlord of the Ship Inn at Dover was awoken by a frantic Frenchman whose uniform proclaimed him to be a Monarchist and whose news was that Napoleon was dead and Paris about to fall to the allies. The glad tidings were duly rushed to London and next morning the Stock Exchange witnessed scenes of unprecedented activity as Government Stocks soared to an all-time high. By lunch-time the market was steadying. There had been no confirmation of the news and the Frenchman had disappeared; in the afternoon confidence ebbed and stocks plummeted. Punters rash and credulous had lost heavily but a small group of men, Cochrane-Johnstone prominent amongst them, had sold out at midday and made a killing. In the subsequent inquiry fraud was fully substantiated. Cochrane-Johnstone, the inspiration behind the hoax, was tried and found guilty. True to form, he fled the country rather than face imprisonment; he never returned.

Meanwhile young John Dundas had been serving with distinction in operations against the French in the north Atlantic. By the age of twenty-one he had risen to the rank of Captain and looked set fair to live down the stigma of his birth. But it was one thing to be illegitimate; another to have for a father the most notorious swindler in living memory. As soon as the Stock Exchange Fraud was substantiated John Dundas obtained leave from the Admiralty and went for a long solitary walk. He tramped round France, Spain and Portugal sleeping rough and taxing his physique to the utmost. Perhaps it was a kind of expiation; perhaps he just relished the anonymity.

The journey which in 1820 found him in St Petersburg was more ambitious but no less unconventional. He had served five more years in the Navy; then peace with France reduced the opportunities for promotion; and he could no longer expect favours from his cousins. A new course needed to be set and, as befitted a Cochrane, it could be challenging.

His first choice had been West Africa, The White Man's Grave. He had read Mungo Park's account of his first terrible odyssey in the African interior and had recognised a kindred spirit. Park's disappearance in 1805 had left the mystery of the River Niger's course and of its navigational possibilities as dark as ever. Cochrane would resume his quest. Of proven stamina, used to tropical conditions, and with the nautical experience necessary for assessing the river's potential, he seemed ideally equipped for the task.

Perhaps the Admiralty agreed. But they were not interested in the African interior and declined his request to be sent there. Cochrane had to think again.

The example of one of Park's predecessors seems to have provided the new inspiration. John Ledyard, an American, had accidentally poisoned himself in Cairo en route to the Niger. But before that he had sailed with Captain Cook, he had lived amongst the American Indians, and he had attempted an overland journey round the world. It was this last idea which caught Cochrane's fancy. The Navy could hardly be expected to support such a scheme but they had given him two years leave of absence and on Monday,

February 14, 1820 – St Valentine's Day and his birthday –
he had strode out of Dieppe heading for London by the
long way round – via, that is, Paris, Berlin, St Petersburg,
Moscow, Siberia, Alaska, Hudsons Bay, Quebec, and
possibly Dublin.

Although unqualified to undertake any scholarly inquiries,
he was keen, like most travellers, to invest this scheme with a
veneer of scientific respectability. He therefore proclaimed
that it was his intention first to establish once and for all
whether the continents of Asia and America were joined at
their Arctic extremities, and then to complement Captain
Parry's work in search of the North-West Passage by following
the frozen shores of America's northern coastline. Yet these
diversions were as nothing compared to the proud boast on
which his celebrity rests. For, to reduce expenses, he
announced that he would walk the whole way.

And walk he had, excluding a short ride in Lithuania and
that lift with the negro from Narva. It was one thousand six
hundred miles from London to St Petersburg. With delays for
borders, blisters, a sprained ankle and some minimal sightseeing, they had taken him eighty-three days. That was an
average of nearly twenty miles a day. He was getting into his
stride; with the wide open spaces of Russia ahead he could
expect to do even better.

Formalities in the Russian capital took three weeks. While
the police were simply suspicious, the Foreign Ministry, and
in particular the Tsar, were incredulous. The Captain's humble, indeed dishevelled, appearance vouched for his story and
the British Consul-General vouched for his identity. But why
should an officer and a gentleman travel on foot? And how
could anyone guarantee his safety if he insisted on behaving as
a vagrant? 'I, however, adhered to one simple story,' explained Cochrane, 'stating as my object a wish to employ,
amuse and improve myself, at the same time rendering to
society all the services of which I was capable.' What services
he had in mind remained a mystery. But the Russian authorities concluded that they, and he, were harmless. Supplied
with the necessary documentation he left St Petersburg on the

47

evening of May 24 and 'with my knapsack on my back trotted over a partially cultivated countryside'.

Rows of silver birch lined the road, their young waxen leaves waving in the breeze. It was as if they had come to see him off. With night falling he climbed the Poulkousky hill and paused by a spring to bid farewell to civilisation. The city's lights twinkled in the distance, stars dotted a cloudless sky, and just for once 'nature here got the better of a tolerably stout heart'. Introspection was not yet a fashionable ingredient in travel writing. Mungo Park had been destitute, naked, lost and half dead before he ventured a few well-chosen words of personal dismay. Cochrane was of the same no-nonsense school. The narrative, not the narrator, was what mattered. Like Park's, his story was to have 'nothing to recommend it but *truth*'. Yet, as a full moon slipped above the horizon, for the first and only time the enormity of his undertaking overwhelmed him. Was he indeed deranged, 'under the baneful influence of that beautiful luminary', as people kept telling him? He smiled – or was it a nervous laugh? – 'and sitting down I read to myself a few lessons which the time and the occasion seemed to inspire'.

'Go,' said I, 'and wander with the illiterate almost brutal savage! Go and be the companion of the ferocious beast! Go and contemplate the human being in every element and climate, whether civilised or savage, of whatever tribe, nation or religion. Make due allowance for the rusticity of their manners; nor be tempted to cope with them in those taunts, insults and rudeness to which the nature of thy enterprise will subject thee ... Should robbers attack thee, do not by a foolish resistance endanger thy life; man is still a humane being even while seeking his subsistence by rapine and plunder; and seldom from mere wantonness will he spill the blood of a fellow creature. It is only by patience, perseverance, and humility, by reducing thyself to the lowest level of mankind, that thou canst expect to pass through the ordeal with either safety or satisfaction.'

Such sentiments were again precisely those of Mungo Park during his first solitary sojourn in Africa. Pulling rank or wealth on savages was unfair and dangerous; survival depended on complete acquiescence; only by experiencing and accepting an alien way of life could one hope to understand it and perhaps learn from it. The early nineteenth-century traveller owed more to Rousseau than to Macaulay. His sentiments as expressed by Park and Cochrane were as remote from those of the Victorians as are our own.

Admirable in many ways, they were also highly demanding, as Cochrane was about to discover. In civilised Europe he had already encountered much incivility. Near Leipzig an innkeeper with a hunched back, a club foot, long matted hair, and a voice like a screech-owl had lived up to his unprepossessing appearance by locking Cochrane in a shed with neither food nor bed; he had eventually escaped through the window. In Berlin the only lodging on offer had been a park bench; a still worse night had found him marooned in an estuary near Königsberg when the ferry became frozen into the ice.

With a bone-chilling breeze blowing from the north his first night out of St Petersburg could have been equally dismal. But at midnight as he cast about for a suitable bivouac, the countryside was suddenly illuminated by a mighty conflagration. Tsarsko Selo, the Tsar's favourite retreat, was going up in flames. He hastened to offer his services as a firefighter. When they were declined he sought out a mossy dell in the palace gardens and dossed down. His only complaint was that the heat gave him nightmares.

Next morning he breakfasted with Prince Theodore Galitsin – who, as one of the palace's stricken inmates, might have preferred not to have to entertain him – and then continued along the road to Moscow. He spent the second night in a peasant's cottage in Tosna and, at the ninth milestone beyond, he sat down for a smoke. Tobacco was one of his few extravagances, but it was not a taste to be indulged indiscriminately. He depended on the sun and the magnifying power of his spectacles for a light; and after arrest in Poland for smoking in the streets, he chose his moment carefully. Today the sun was strong, not a soul was in sight, and his tobacco pouch was full. He even had a few cigars. It was while he was quietly debating whether to go for his pipe or a Havana that he was suddenly seized from behind.

His assailant, with an iron bar in one hand and the scruff of the Captain's neck in the other, was endeavouring to drag him away from the road. Another man followed close behind with a musket and bayonet which he employed 'in such a manner as to make me move with more than ordinary celerity'. Stooping they scuttled deep into the silence of the forest. 'There I was desired to undress.' Trousers, jacket, shirt, shoes and stockings were removed and the victim tied to a tree. 'From this ceremony I concluded that they intended to try the effect of a musket upon me by firing at me as they would at a mark.' But not so. Instead they sat down and proceeded to rifle through his scanty belongings. Except for a jacket and a couple of waistcoats, they appropriated all his clothes, plus his watch, spectacles, compass, thermometer and cash; the last came to the equivalent of about £7. Perhaps by way of compensation they then proceeded to stuff their victim with about two pounds of black bread plus the contents of his flask. Then at knife point they extracted a promise from him that he would not inform on them – 'such, at least, I conjectured to be their meaning though of their language I understood not a word' – and departed.

Cochrane waited; then shouted. His cries were heard by a small boy who duly released him. Unharmed, although 'almost as naked as the day I came into the world', he regained the road. Compliance had paid off. He would have been positively grateful for such a vindication of his philosophy if only the robbers had had the decency to leave him a pair of trousers.

To pursue my route or to return to Tsarsko Selo would indeed be alike indecent and ridiculous; but there being no remedy, I made 'forward' the order of the day; and having first with the remnant of my apparel rigged myself *á l'Écossaise* I resumed my route. I had still left me a blue jacket, a flannel waistcoat, and a spare one; the latter I tied round my waist in such a way that it reached down to my knees. My empty knapsack was restored to its old place and I trotted on with even a merry heart.

Although now barefoot, he rather liked his makeshift kilt and refused the first offer of new clothes. There was just no limit to people's generosity when they descried such a woebegone wayfarer. For two days he shuffled on, footsore but well fed, and reached the old capital of Novgorod in time for Whit Sunday. Here he did accept from the Governor a complete refit plus an advance against the recovery of his cash.

Novgorod was the first town in Muscovy. He immediately spotted a change in the appearance of the womenfolk. Though not unattractive they 'disfigure themselves by the abominable custom of tying their breasts as low, flat, and tight as possible'. They looked only slightly less ridiculous than the Creole women in the West Indies who, he recalled, 'often suckle their children behind their backs'.

At the next town, Torzhok, he took refuge from a thunderstorm in the inn and was there accosted by a teenage widow who was none other than 'the sister of the Captain Golovnin who was so inhumanly exposed in a cage in Japan'. She spoke excellent English, was deliciously sympathetic, 'and so got all of my secrets out of me but one'. The one she did not get was presumably that Cochrane was smitten. When she offered to relieve his poverty with a few roubles he declined, 'but had she offered me her heart and hand I would certainly have replied otherwise'. Love at first sight was one of his few weaknesses; ultimately it would prove his undoing.

Two days later he reached Tver (now Kalinin) and there resolved on a final dash for Moscow.

Early on Monday June 5 I quitted Tver . . . reached Davidova (32 miles) by two o'clock where I stopped to refresh . . . at eight in the evening I continued my route, reaching Klinn at midnight and Peski at four in the morning . . . passing through Tschornaya Graz I entered Moscow at eight in the morning, the last stage being distressingly fatiguing . . . The last thirty-two hours I warrant as bearing witness to one of my greatest pedestrian trips – the distance is 168 versts, or about 96 miles.

On such feats Cochrane's reputation as 'The Pedestrian Traveller' would rest. Ninety-six miles in thirty-two hours was not a record; he had done the same in Portugal. But it does raise an interesting question: did he walk or run? Next day, sightseeing in Moscow, he crawled inside the barrel of the city's mammoth cannon. This was a standard tourist prank. But Cochrane records that he was able to sit upright inside it, which was not standard. His stature must indeed have been 'lilly' and therefore his stride short. When he writes of 'trotting' or 'jogging' he may mean it literally.

But against this must be set the fact that often he moved in the company of other travellers – carters, students, war veterans and, on one occasion, 'a wandering tailor, a regenerator of kettles and an Italian cage-maker'. Such people presumably had a more leisurely pace; it is hard, for instance, to imagine a regenerator of kettles travelling at a trot. Additionally neither Cochrane's feet nor his footwear were in a fit state for running. From one of his casual companions, a man who had marched to Moscow with Napoleon, then on to Siberia as a prisoner of war, and then back to Europe, he had picked up a useful tip about blisters.

It is simply to rub the feet at going to bed with spirits mixed with tallow dropped from a lighted candle. The spirit seems to possess the healing power, the tallow serving only to keep the skin soft and pliant. The soles of the feet, ankles and insteps should be rubbed well even where no blisters exist. Salt and water is a good substitute.

But sometimes he neglected the treatment and sometimes his shoes got the better of it. He had come to the conclusion that shoes with a left and a right foot were unnatural and uneconomical; they cramped the feet and wore out too quickly. Better by far were roomy ambidextrous models which could be swapped to even out the wear. Such a pair had taken him most of the way across Europe and he had continued to swear by them even when they were reduced to a pulpy blotting paper and had to be tied on with string. As such they were, of course, quite useless for running. One must assume, then, that Cochrane's normal pace was that of an urgent walk, that his stride was short and rapid, and his gait springy with perhaps a slight nautical roll. At a distance he might have appeared like something clockwork and overwound.

Eight days sufficed for Moscow. He rattled round the sights but, as in most other places, excused himself from describing them on the grounds that others had already done so. With the city still being rebuilt after its sack by Napoleon, there was indeed less at which to marvel. 'On the 30th of May,' he writes, 'I quitted Moscow.'

Since he had just admitted to arriving on June 7, reviewers of his book would be puzzled by this statement. Throughout his travels in the Russian empire only half a dozen more dates would be mentioned. If he could be so unreliable about chronology, why should his itinerary not be equally suspect? But Cochrane had a ready explanation. Russia used the old calendar. Some of his dates were old style, some new. He himself had become so confused that he had meant to remove dates from his narrative altogether. Needless to say, such a cavalier attitude did not endear him to the scientific establishment at home. It was a small matter but indicative of an impatient and obtuse streak in the Captain's character.

East of Moscow the towns became fewer, the distances greater and the days hotter. Mostly he travelled at night resting up during the middle of the day in a barn, under a bridge or, once, in a barrel. At Nijni Novgorod (now Gorkiy) he made his preference clear by spurning the offer of a bed in order to sleep in his host's garden. But the outdoor life was doing nothing for his appearance. When he went to call on the wife of the Governor, an Englishwoman, he was taken for a vagabond and sent packing.

From Nijni Novgorod the river Volga flowed east to Kazan. 'On a freak of fancy' he decided to pass this next stage as a boatman. In return for acting as ship's cook and keeping the skipper supplied with vodka he was given free passage on a barge which covered the two hundred miles in twelve days. 'To make up for lost time' he then accepted a lift in a carriage from Kazan to Perm, at least three hundred miles. He was, of course, cheating. But the nearer he came to Siberia, the greater his willingness to compromise. Slowly the whole character of his journey was beginning to change. In Europe his travels would have been unremarkable had he not insisted on walking; in Asia they would be sufficiently demanding and notable however he chose to prosecute them.

He still preferred to walk whenever possible. On foot again as he left Perm, he rejoiced in the easy going through fertile valleys 'nursed in the bosom of peace and fed with the abundance of plenty'. They comprised the foothills of the Ural mountains and their pastoral calm was all the gayer for preceding the Siberian wastes on the other side. Cochrane was understandably apprehensive about Siberia. No British traveller had yet traversed more than half its enormous length; but its reputation for severity and misery, for cold and convicts, was even grimmer than it is today.

At noon sometime in the middle of July he breasted the main mountain chain. On the pass the air was freezing. But the gradient was gentle enough and a mob of small children kept him well supplied with strawberries and cream.

The strawberries were of an excellent flavour and it is the custom of these poor people to present the traveller with such fruit during the season. I received the present standing with one foot in Asia and the other in Europe, surrounded on all sides by lofty mountains covered, however, with nothing but brushwood.

Back in the dense and uninterrupted pine forests he pounded down and on. Far from being hostile, Siberia proved unexpectedly hospitable. 'I never entered a cottage but shtshee (a cabbage soup) with meat, milk and bread were placed before me unasked.' Greatly relieved at being spared what he called 'the unsocial and hackeneyed custom of paying for food' he consigned his purse to the bottom of his knapsack and proclaimed Siberia a pauper's paradise.

In fact, of course, it was a paradise only for one armed with the credentials and directives that he had secured from the Tsar's ministers in St Petersburg. The Captain was undoubtedly hard up and therefore happy to take advantage of his privileged position. But those of his readers who complained that such free-loading brought his rank and his nation into disrepute, failed to understand local custom. In Siberia no one paid his way; all travellers were either convicts or accredited government servants. Perhaps his critics were simply suspicious because he was the son of the awful Cochrane-Johnstone. Yet far from emulating his father's fraudulent ways, John Dundas was, if anything, trying to disassociate himself from them. Here is a Cochrane, he seemed to be saying, who will starve rather than steal and beg rather than cheat.

Through Ekaterineburg (now Sverdlovsk) to Tobolsk and then Omsk, he averaged thirty miles a day in spite of three-day halts in each. He now had the obligatory services of a Cossack guard and the option of commandeering a horse when available. The former he regretted bitterly – the man kept getting left behind; the latter he mostly eschewed. Like a straining hound slipped from its leash, he now shook off the constraints of civilised Europe and began to course the wide open spaces of Siberia glorying in their mere extent.

For some travellers distance is an irrelevance. Each day's journey is a happy paper-chase from one novelty to the next; adventure awaits them in the most prosaic places; their notebooks are filled while their boots are yet un-scuffed. At the opposite extreme there are those who suspend all observation until half-way round the world and deep into virgin territory. For them remoteness is everything, and however little may befall them there its value and interest is undeniable simply because it is happening a very long way away. A letter from Yarkand, say, does not need to be exciting; anything from Yarkand simply has to be worth reading.

John Dundas Cochrane fitted neither of these categories. Whether in Calais or Kamchatka he was ever sparing with the details. Geographical features and political frontiers were just inconveniences, cities mere milestones. For Cochrane what mattered was locomotion. To feel the furlongs ticking away and the miles slipping behind was his greatest joy. Like a man on the run his destination was irrelevant. But so was his starting point. His ambition was simply to prove himself and to test his constitution, 'the like of which', he wrote with some truth and much pride, 'I have never seen equalled'.

And what better proving ground for this marvel of loco-motion than the wastes of Siberia? If there was little to see, so much the better. He could concentrate exclusively on the sensation of travel itself. From Omsk, instead of continuing east along the main trans-Siberian route, he struck south on the first of two marathon detours. Following the river Irtysh he reached Semipalatinsk in Kazakhstan and then continued south-east heading for the Russian frontier with Chinese

Sinkiang. The forest gave way to steppe and the steppe to semi-desert. Instead of peasant cottages he now dined in the yurts of Calmack and Kirghiz herdsmen. There were few towns; the staging posts were all mud forts garrisoned by Cossack troops. Increasingly he accepted a ride between them.

At last, some six hundred miles from his starting point in Omsk, the first hills since the Urals broke the horizon. Broad and level valleys covered in lush grazing wound in amongst them. Cochrane thought this forgotten corner of Russia on the edge of the Altai mountains the most picturesque and promising he had seen. But lacking 'a poetical imagination', he knew better than to attempt its description. At midnight, after a long climb, he at last stood on the Chinese frontier. Obligingly the moon bathed both scene and occasion in a ghostly significance.

Apparently full, she was near her meridian and seemed to encourage a pensive inclination. What can surpass that scene I know not. Some of the loftiest granite mountains spreading in various directions, enclosing some of the most luxuriant valleys in the world. Yet all deserted! – all this fair and fertile tract abandoned to wild beasts, merely to constitute a neutral territory.

Two weeks later, having made the return journey mainly by canoe, he was back on the trans-Siberian road at the mining town of Barnaul. Here his path crossed with that of General Speranski, Governor-General of Siberia. At first the General mistook the traveller for a member of the heretical Raskolnick sect; presumably it was because of 'my long beard and even longer golden locks'. Apologies were forthcoming and Cochrane was entered on the guest list for the round of picnics, dinners and balls which marked the Governor-General's visit. 'I of course shone a conspicuous object.' He had now adopted Central Asian costume consisting of a long grey nankeen dressing-gown tied with a silk sash. What with the beard and the long golden locks he must have resembled a small apostle.

The impression was evidently favourable. Speranski became his friend and patron, and it was on his suggestion that Cochrane made his next detour into the unknown.

He told me that there was an expedition on the river Kolyma fitted out to solve the question regarding the north east cape of Asia; and His Excellency kindly offered me his permission to proceed with it. Too glad to accept a favour of the kind I instantly closed with it and determined not to waste a moment in Irkutsk and Yakutsk but to proceed immediately to the Frozen Sea.

The Frozen Sea was the Arctic Ocean; the Kolyma river is in about the same longitude as New Zealand; and from Barnaul it was as far away as London. Undismayed by the prospect of a four-thousand-mile hike, Cochrane immediately headed east. Tomsk, on the Tom, was notable for the fact that he left it on the Tsar's name day – that meant it was August 30 – Krasnoyarsk for its mosquitoes, and Irkutsk, the capital of Eastern Siberia, for its lively society. A hundred and fifty miles beyond, 'the communication by land ceases, a circumstance at which I was not a little rejoiced'. He transferred to a canoe and with a Cossack companion paddled off down the River Lena heading now north with a further one thousand five hundred miles to Yakutsk. Travelling day and night and with the current in his favour, he 'generally made 100 to 120 miles during each day's progress'. The stream wound through a maze of islands between densely wooded shores. Settlements of Russian colonists, each with its little oasis of fields, provided the only relief and the only chance of obtaining provisions. They were, in effect, staging posts.

Cochrane's breakneck speed was soon explained. It must have been about mid-September. The days were drawing in and the cold increasing. At a place called Vittim they encountered their first ice floes. The forests had been left behind and the early snows fell on desolate pastures. Two days short of Yakutsk the canoe was finally frozen into the ice and abandoned. They waded ashore through the ice floes – 'no pleasant circumstance with 12–15 degrees of Reaumur's frost' – and rode into Yakutsk on October 6 (by Julian's calendar, presumably).

Here he was delayed for three weeks waiting for winter to assert its grip and the river to be declared safe for sledges. He stayed with the Governor of the place, a naval officer who had once served with the Royal Navy and therefore, inevitably, with a Cochrane. From this man he gained some insight into the perils that still lay ahead of him.

My destination was Nishney [Nijni] Kolymsk, distant one thousand eight hundred miles which were to be travelled over in the coldest season of the year in what is esteemed the coldest part of north-east Asia. All this I heeded nothing and provided, as I thought, with warm clothing, considered myself as proof against at least 50 degrees of frost. The spirit thermometer at Yakutsk was 27 degrees below zero Fahrenheit yet I walked about the streets with only my nankeen surtout, trousers of the same material, shoes and worsted stockings. A flannel waistcoat which had lost its principal virtue was the only warm clothing. Yet I can truly say that I was not at all incommoded.

It was true that the local people regarded his situation as 'forlorn and hopeless'; but they failed to make allowances for his resolve. 'When mind and body are in constant motion, the elements can have little effect upon the person.' So long as there was 'a shot in the locker' he would never shrink from 'the point of duty'. And thanks to 'a solid education' he insisted that he was 'never happier than when encountering these difficulties'. Accordingly he took his preparations lightly – indeed a little too lightly.

I had no second parka, or frock; no knee-preservers, blanket or bed; an indifferent pair of gloves and a cold cap; no guard for my chin, ears or nose; in short I was not properly provided, which I found out too late.

Thanks to his host he was better equipped in the matter of provisions. Although two bags of black biscuit, a piece of roast beef, some dried fish, six pounds of tea and twenty pounds of sugar candy constituted a modest commissariat by any standards but Cochrane's, he also took a keg of vodka and fifty pounds of tobacco which could be exchanged with the eskimo tribes for more meat and fish. 'I had besides a pipe, flint, steel and axe and, what was of more importance, a Cossack companion who for once proved invaluable.' He could not of course converse with the Cossack, nor with any of the Eskimos, nor with the Russian settlers unless they happened to have a smattering of French. But communication was the least of his problems.

On the day his two horse-drawn sledges pulled out onto the

frozen river the thermometer showed twenty degrees of frost. Never did it get any higher. It was so cold sitting on the sledge that Cochrane preferred to walk and run behind it. After a couple of days his face was shredded. At night they crawled inside a Yakuti hut. But when they left the river and began to climb across country even this comfort was denied them. Each evening they excavated a two-foot hollow in the snow, filled it with branches by way of bedding, and lit a fire in the middle. 'We then put the kettle on and soon forgot the sufferings of the day.' Instead there were the sufferings of the night. They were accompanied by guides of the Yakuti tribe, the most numerous of the Siberian Eskimos. The Yakutis kept Cochrane well supplied with meat but had an irritating habit of drawing the fire to their own side of the hollow as soon as he fell asleep. Considering that he was much the worst provided for clothes, and therefore had to get up every few hours and leap about to release his circulation, this could not continue. Accordingly he pioneered the 'horseshoe shaped fire'. Positioning himself inside the horseshoe he at last got a sound night's sleep.

Floundering up ever steeper hills through ever deeper snow they managed to walk, ride and slide about twenty miles a day. Meanwhile the temperature sank to thirty degrees below freezing. Survival depended on steady progress but the effort involved was enough to make even Cochrane wonder whether it was worth it. 'But go I must for return I would not had things been ten times worse.' The agonies of snow-blindness he ascribed to the weight of snow accumulating on the eyelashes. And his blistered feet were the result not, he thought, of insufficient embrocation with candle grease but of drops of sweat repeatedly freezing on the skin. His knees were also giving trouble. They did not actually feel cold but they were quite numb and increasingly stiff. Without realising it, he was suffering from frostbite. Happily a passing traveller with a few words of French diagnosed the problem and prescribed knee-preservers made of reindeer skin.

The service they did me was astonishing. From that moment I had less pain and more heat, and became fully satisfied that the extremities alone are to be taken care of. The golden rule, which I have never found to err, is always to follow the example and customs of the natives. Whether in a hot, cold or temperate climate, they ought to know what is most necessary or proper.

This dictum also applied to food. When the Yakutis brought down a massive elk he was immediately presented with what they considered its greatest delicacy – the bone marrow of the front legs, uncooked and still warm. 'I did not find it disagreeable.' If raw meat was acceptable, raw fish was pure ambrosia. Oysters, clotted cream or the finest jelly in the world could not touch it. On occasion he would eat a whole fish weighing three pounds after gutting, 'and with black biscuit and a glass of rye brandy I defy either nature or art to prepare a better meal'.

Only in the matter of quantity could he never match the example of the Yakutis. Repeatedly he watched one of their number devour an incredible forty pounds of meat, raw or putrid, in a single day. Three men would polish off a whole reindeer at one sitting. 'The effect is very observable upon them for from thin and meagre looking men they become perfectly pot-bellied.' In a Yakuti home he encountered a child, not more than five years old, whose appetite convinced him that these people must have a totally different digestive system.

I had observed the child crawling upon the floor and scraping up with its thumb the grease which fell from a lighted candle. I enquired in surprise whether it proceeded from hunger or from a liking for fat. Neither, I was told, simply from the habit of eating whenever there is food. I then gave the child a candle made of the most impure tallow – then a second – then a third; all were devoured with avidity. My Cossack companion then gave him several pounds of sour frozen butter. These also he immediately consumed. Lastly a large piece of yellow soap went the same way. I was now convinced that the child would continue to gorge as long as it could receive anything and I begged my companion to desist.

Such moments of light relief were to be treasured. In late November they crossed into the Arctic Circle and Cochrane's peregrination, begun as an eccentric jaunt, became a dour polar slog. The snow was now six feet deep and the horses proving more hindrance than help. In each drift they had to be unloaded, dug out, and then reloaded. On the rivers the ice was so smooth that even with rags tied round their hooves they slithered and crashed to the floor. One died, another had to be abandoned.

At last they descended to a vast snow desert and met their first dog-sleds. The plain presaged the ocean and journey's end. After a Christmas dinner consisting of a wolf and a horse 'which the day before had fought one another to the death', they embarked on the final leg; and on New Year's Eve, 'after a tedious, laborious, and to me perilous journey [from Yakutsk] of 61 days, and 20 nights in the snow without even the comfort of a blanket – a great oversight', Cochrane reached Nijni Kolymsk. He immediately introduced himself to the Russian expedition that was wintering there and to Baron Wrangel, its leader. He joined in the Hogmanay celebrations and did not refuse the offer of a bed in the Baron's house. 'And with him, on the shores of the Frozen Ocean, I enjoyed health and every comfort I could desire.'

It was not, however, a particularly happy New Year. Having come four thousand miles specifically to join the expedition, he was politely informed that without the permission of the Tsar himself it was out of the question. To get that permission a message would have to be sent to St Petersburg. No reply could be expected before the summer yet the expedition was to move out onto the polar ice-cap in February.

Cochrane took the news with surprisingly good grace. If he could not join an official expedition he could still conduct his own inquiries. With a view to following the Arctic coastline to its termination at the Bering Strait he determined to make contact with the Chukchi Eskimos who inhabited this extremity of Siberia and on whose services any such progress would depend.

In the early nineteenth century the Russian empire had no definable eastern frontier. The Tsar's rule simply petered out into unclaimed wastes of frozen ocean and snowy tundra. Although there were mariners who claimed to have passed through the Bering Strait – and whom Cochrane for one believed – it did seem inherently improbable that two such enormous land masses as Asia and America should come to within about fifty miles of one another and not join up. The notion that the Strait was just an inlet, and that somewhere to the north, through the fogs and the ice, the two continents finally united, was tenacious and challenging. It also put the question of political frontiers in a very different light. Administratively Nijni Kolymsk was Russia's last outpost in the north-east and the Chukchi lands enjoyed as much autonomy as did the Inuit lands in Alaska. But commercially the Imperial tentacles reached much further and through far-flung trading posts a vague authority was claimed over both sides of the Bering Strait.

Typical of this commercial activity and of its political undertones was the Chukchi Fair held every February in a snowy waste a hundred and fifty miles to the east of Nijni Kolymsk. On the appointed spot Chukchi sledges converged laden with furs and pulled by reindeer, while from the west came Russian and Cossack traders huddled in their dog-sleds amongst bales of tobacco. In 1821 the Russian Commissary in charge opened proceedings with the usual formalities. Presents were exchanged and a family of Chukchis, men and women, were dunked stark naked in a barrel of water. This was by way of baptism, a customary concession to Mother Russia's evangelising conscience; the Chukchi girls emerged with their hair tinkling with icicles but the gifts that went with this ceremony were such that the same family habitually came forward for conversion each year. Then, via his interpreter, the Commissary made an unusual request. He wanted the Chukchi to receive a white man, a British sailor who was a friend of the Tsar, and to conduct him to Alaska.

Reasonably enough, the Chukchi asked for further details, then concluded that if the man was really a friend of the Tsar, the Tsar would pay. They demanded the equivalent of fifty thousand pounds of tobacco. To his credit, Cochrane, far from raging over such an exorbitant and impossible demand, was filled with admiration for the savages' acumen. If he could not travel with them he could at least make the most of the fair. Accordingly he spent the next seven days investigating their way of life and probing their knowledge of the region's geography.

On his own admission his *Travels* would contribute little to science. Sure enough the book was dismissed by the Royal Society and ridiculed by patronising reviewers. Yet his observations on the indigenous peoples of Arctic Asia ('indians' or 'eskimos') are colourful, perceptive and unusually detailed. As a general principle Cohrane's respect for those amongst whom he passed rose the less they were affected by 'so-called civilisation'. Himself an outsider with nothing to boast about except his extraordinary physique, he felt a natural sympathy with those whose cause was unfashionable, way of life basic and environment harsh. And no peoples better fitted this description than the Yakuti, Yukagir, Chukchi and Tungoose. For many of his readers – now as then – his narrative would provide the first introduction to their existence. Yet each of these 'tribes' was distinct with its own peculiar dress, transport, hunting methods and food pattern. Their origins too he thought were different. The Yakuti, for instance, seemed to be of Chinese stock, while the Chukchi, because of their language and their disdain of chess, he took to be of American or Inuit origin. He was no anthropologist but his observations of peoples who were even then threatened with assimilation and who have since succumbed completely, deserved, and deserve, closer study.

Instead his critics concentrated on the supposed extravagances of his narrative. Temperatures as low as minus eighty degrees Fahrenheit (or minus fifty Réaumur) were declared to be wild exaggerations. So was his account of two afflictions common amongst the inhabitants of the Arctic Circle. One was convulsive hiccoughs; it affected pregnant women and was invariably fatal. The other was a medical oddity called imerachism which compelled anyone suffering from it to imitate whatever was said or done in his presence. Thus a knock at the door would set the imerach pummelling the walls, a glimpse of dogs would start him barking and growling, and an encounter with a bear would make him roar and dance. It was never fatal and 'carried with it an air of merriment'.

But nothing would strain his readers' credulity more than

the account of his last major undertaking in Siberia. Blocked in his further progress east and north, he elected to head south for the Pacific port of Okhotsk, there to seek a passage to Alaska or to the Kamchatkan peninsula. The plan was sensible enough but to avoid retracing his steps to Yakutsk he chose a cross-country route which, though more direct, lay entirely through trackless mountains. To attempt such a route in the spring, the most dangerous time of the year in any mountains, was sheer madness. 'But I was resolutely fixed upon the new route and the result will show that I had only myself to thank for the difficuties and the narrow escapes I had so often for my life.'

Although, thanks to Baron Wrangel, he was better provided for in terms of clothing, horses and companions, he did not exaggerate. The thousand miles to Okhotsk took seventy-five days of gruesome travail. Forty-five nights were spent in the snow, often without fire in thirty degrees of frost. Yet by day the temperature might soar into the seventies. Where the snow and ice had been crisp and dry on the journey north, they were now soft, wet, and treacherous. On one pass they were marooned for three days as they hacked a staircase up the ice and then carpeted it with earth to make a safe ascent for the horses. The horses still suffered appallingly and when the sixth succumbed they changed to reindeer. These too proved unequal to the deep snow and the now thundering rivers. Most of the baggage had to be sacrificed; for weeks on end they ate nothing but horsemeat and venison; when even these ran out they ate nothing at all for five days.

Cochrane tells his tale simply. Only its sheer horror strains belief. Near journey's end he builds a raft; they career down river in the midst of uprooted tree-trunks and bobbing icebergs, then collide with an island. The raft does a nose-dive. Cochrane is swept a hundred yards downstream and marooned in the branches of a fallen tree. He scrambles back to the island and begins to improvise a pontoon bridge by lashing tree trunks together. In pitch darkness his Yakuti companions somehow manage to teeter across. Cochrane, going last, is again swept away. He emerges from the torrent still alive but paralysed, his clothes having frozen into an icy straitjacket. The Yakutis light a fire to thaw him out which immediately gets out of hand. He is saved from cremation only because he is still too wet to burn. And so on. From any other traveller such a headlong narrative would indeed be suspect. But from Cochrane it rings true. 'The difficulties', he wrote, 'surpassed everything of the kind I have before seen.' Given what he had before seen – and survived – this was no hollow boast.

Perhaps more suspect were the reasons he now advanced for giving up his plan of crossing to Alaska and completing his circuit of the world. At Okhotsk, he explains, he learnt that another Russian expedition was even then probing Alaska's north coast. 'I cannot be allowed to act with them . . . ; I will not act against them; and therefore I cannot act at all.' Ever sensitive about the rights of explorers, he seemed quite happy to accept that the Russians had again pre-empted him. But that need not have stopped him from crossing. At one point he hints that he was refused any passage to Alaska; at another that he could not afford to wait for one. His reasoning is confused and unconvincing. And there are two other possible explanations.

One is that he was simply running out of steam. The clockwork was unwinding, the locker almost bare. The last marathon from Nijni Kolymsk had taken a heavy toll of his confidence. He was lucky to be alive and knew it. The risk was not one he would want to take again, the achievement not one that he could expect to repeat. Surely he had done enough to prove himself.

But another and more persuasive reason for the change of plan emerges later. From Okhotsk he did not in fact head for home but continued east, taking a passage to the port of Petropavlovsk on the Kamchatka peninsula. Evidently he still thought there might be a chance of reaching Alaska. In Petropavlovsk he found most of the Russian Alaska expedition, plus a Portuguese brig from Macao and another, somewhat improbably, from the Sandwich Islands. 'The former brought a cargo of flour, the latter a cargo of salt, a

present to the Tsar from the sable Majesty of those islands.'
The wisdom of sending salt to Siberia escaped his comment;
but he was delighted to find the ship officered by three
Englishmen. To celebrate such an international congregation
of shipping in these little-frequented waters 'balls, routs,
dinners and masquerades' succeeded one another in a dizzy
round. Cochrane himself hosted one such gathering 'when
for the first time the British flag waved over the land of
Kamchatka'. But if this evidence of gracious living seems
somewhat out of character, it does little to prepare the reader
for the sentence that follows.

Two months passed in this manner before the [Russian] expedition departed, when I was left to the free enjoyment of a passion that was crowned
with marriage; – so much then for my travellership. However, I had no
alternative, and the day that Captain Vassilieff [leader of the expedition]
left the harbour of Petropavlovsk, I put the question.

Obliquely phrased, coming somewhere around page 300, and
all but smothered between sundry remarks on the Kurile
Islands and the start of his next ramble, this development is
easily missed by the weary reader. Cochrane evidently wanted
it thus. Perhaps he felt that it lowered the tone of his narrative,
or that this evidence of emotional frailty was inconsistent with
his physical prowess. But why was there 'no alternative'? Had
he compromised the young lady in some way? And why was
his proposal dependent on the departure of the Russian
expedition? Was he hoping until the very last that they might
offer him a passage and so an escape from wedlock? Who,
indeed, was this lady of charms so persuasive that she could
terminate his travellership? Cochrane chose not to say.

My airy phantoms, my bold desires, and my eccentric turn being thus
dissipated by one woman, I prepared to make a tour of the [Kamchatka]
peninsula before I led my intended bride to the altar.

His travellership was not over. The peregrination of the
Kamchatka peninsula, although subdued and even boring,
took several months. He then returned to Petropavlovsk,
married, and stayed on for a further nine months. Husband
and wife then sailed back to Okhotsk and went by sledge to

Yakutsk and Irkutsk whence Cochrane made another excursion to the Chinese frontier. They then continued west, travelling now in some style, and reached Moscow in May 1823.

Here their path crossed with that of James Holman, himself en route for Siberia and no less a travelling phenomenon than Cochrane; for if Cochrane was The Pedestrian Traveller, Holman was The Blind Traveller. Notwithstanding this disability, Holman took Mrs Cochrane to the theatre. She was fourteen years old, he reported, small, shy and pretty, and the daughter of a Kamchatkan chief; the performance, however, was beyond her.

Holman was right about her age and her appearance. An engraving shows a demure and décolletée nymph, fashionably long necked and with eyes slightly slanted. To the extent that she had been born in the village of Bolcheretsk she was certainly a native of Kamchatka. According to the historian of the Cochrane clan her father was 'Vladimir Ushinsky, a Kamchatkan chief'. But Cochrane himself describes the village as being inhabited entirely by Russians. And the editor of the Third Edition of his *Travels* (published in 1829) states unequivocally that she was the daughter of Captain Rikord, the Russian Governor of Kamchatka – and therefore 'a lady' and not, as one reviewer had labelled her, 'a Kamchatka girl'. The confusion probably stems from Cochrane's habit of describing provincial governors as 'chiefs'. If he so described Captain Rikord he did not mean to imply that the Captain was the head of an Eskimo clan.

The groom's failure to reveal the name or paternity of his wife is not altogether surprising. With the marriage over he scarcely mentions her existence. But he certainly thought well of Captain Rikord and it may be significant that Mrs Rikord accompanied the newly-weds at least as far as Yakutsk.

Husband and wife eventually took ship from St Petersburg to London in the summer of 1823. What 'the first native of Kamchatka that ever visited happy Britain' made of her changed circumstances would have made a narrative as interesting as her husband's. Curiously in 1830 a certain 'Juan de Vega' would publish just such an account, being the impressions gained by a foreigner, in this case a Spanish minstrel, wandering through the British Isles. 'Juan de Vega' was later revealed to be Captain Charles Stuart Cochrane, one of John Dundas's cousins.

The idea would not have appealed to John Dundas himself. He prided himself on being reserved for sterner stuff; his humour was unconscious. The success of his *Travels* was gratifying but sadly it owed too much to the author's idiosyncrasies and too little to his achievements. He confidently expected that now, having proved his dedication and stamina, the Admiralty, the Government or the scientific world would find some worthy assignment for him. He would leave for Africa, for anywhere, at a minute's notice, he wrote in his book. But nothing materialised.

In June 1824, 'having engaged in some mining speculations in South America', he sailed for Colombia. Mrs Cochrane remained at home. He returned at the end of the year but went again to Colombia in 1825; the ship was called *The Frolic* but it presaged no fortune. Soon after his arrival, on August 12, 1825, at a place called Valencia, he died of fever. Mrs Cochrane returned to Russia and is described as having 'soon met with many admirers'. By 1829 she was remarried and residing at Kronstadt, the port for St Petersburg. Kronstadt is on the Gulf of Finland, fifty miles from Narva – for the greatest pedestrian of the century a comfortable day's walk.

CHAPTER THREE
A WALK ON THE WEIRD SIDE
Dr Ludwig Leichhardt

Diffidence ill becomes the travel writer. A personal narrative has to be personal and its author has to appear prominently; a certain conceit underlies the whole genre. But being gentlemen, MacGregor and Cochrane recognised the need for restraint. Eccentricity was forgivable; egocentricity was not. They both, therefore, began their stories by apologising profusely for writing in the first person singular. Too many 'I's, they recognised, would strain the gentle readers' indulgence.

Cochrane, having identified the problem, failed to find a way round it. But MacGregor was more successful. On stage he had a repertoire of disguises; in print he could be equally ingenious. In mid-chapter he would leap from pronoun to pronoun, jettisonning the objectionable 'I' in favour of 'he' (the canoeist, i.e. MacGregor), then 'we' (the canoeist, i.e. MacGregor plus his canoe), then 'you' (the reader co-opted as apprentice canoeist, i.e. MacGregor the novice) and finally 'one' (canoeists in general but MacGregor in particular). Such manoeuvres, when agilely conducted, had the added bonus of seeming to invite the reader's participation in events as a privileged companion. MacGregor, it was said, 'carries his readers along with him'. So polite and dexterous an author was welcome in any company. He was approachable, likeable, a good fellow.

Literary style would seem to have a lot to do with good manners. The reader likes to be flattered by the company he keeps. Thus, as a general rule, authors who write in the first person do well to appear affable and endearing as well as entertaining. This dictum applies to the savant as well as the popular writer and to the explorer as well as the traveller.

Disregard of it has prejudiced not a few reputations, amongst them that of Friedrich Wilhelm Ludwig Leichhardt.

The most memorable encounter with 'Doctor' Leichhardt is that recorded by one Henry Stuart Russell, a gentleman rancher and pioneer who had staked his claim to a handsome slice of the Darling Downs in Queensland, Australia. The year was 1844, the day was hot, the time mid-afternoon. Russell, in search of shade and tea, was homing in on his cabin beside the Condamine River. Above it a ridge covered in acacia scrub formed one side of his stockyard; and it was there, bobbing about in the topmost thorns, that Russell described a curious object, 'an old-fashioned, tall, black, hat'. It was the sort that undertakers wore and that outlaws put bullets through, 'a veritable chimney-pot'. Beside it a more prosaic 'cabbage tree' made its appearance. Russell recognised the latter; it was Fairholme, one of his neighbours. But whose the black hat? 'Dr Ludwig Leichhardt,' explained the neighbour, where-upon the newcomer raised his chimney-pot and was promptly smothered by its hidden contents.

The fine face was suddenly bespattered with half a bushel of flowers, leaves and vegetable specimens; the hat too was girt round with sundry creepers and climbers, and here and there a beetle [was] speared to the brim.

A botanist, evidently a man of science, surmised Russell. 'An earnest and to all appearances amiable inquirer into the general arcana of nature.' (Russell, an Oxford graduate, liked to alliterate.) And a German. The accent was unmistakable.

As was the custom on the then frontiers of settlement, Russell's guests made themselves at home. They stayed for several days exchanging news. Of an evening they sprawled on the verandah watching their pipesmoke curl into the Outback. Stories were told, anxieties shared, dreams re-vealed. And no story was stranger, no dream more extrava-gant, than that of the botanising Leichhardt.

Born in 1813 in an obscure township in Brandenburg (Prussia), Ludwig Leichhardt had begun his improbable career in unfavoured circumstances. His father was a peasant-farmer whose proudest boast was that he was also 'Herr Torf

Inspektor' – in other words he acted as the town's arbiter in the matter of peat extraction. Young Ludwig, his sixth child, showed aptitude neither for farming nor for peat digging. He was thin and sickly with a long inquisitive nose and poor eyesight. But he was undoubtedly clever, in his own context a veritable prodigy. Greedy for knowledge, immensely hard-working, and anything but diffident about his own genius, he thumbed the books and gratified his teachers. There were expectations that one day he might himself become a school-master or a government servant. To the plodding Leichhardt parents these were prestigious and desirable callings; young Ludwig became the apple of their eye. An aunt was persuaded to fund his attendance at universities in Berlin and Göttingen where he rewarded the family's confidence by working even harder. Classics, then languages, and finally the natural sciences, especially botany, bowed before his scholarship. From his academic eminence he also directed the affairs of his admiring relations. His brothers he advised on their careers, his father he upbraided for not appreciating his now divorced mother. Judged by his letters the young scholar was some-thing of a prig.

Yet his family seem not to have resented his attitude. Nor did they do more than meekly demur when in 1836 he shattered their dreams by abruptly renouncing the university curriculum. 'Away with all that,' he told his father, thus dismissing his chances of a degree, of steady employment, and of reimbursing his family for their sacrifices. He had other ideas; he would devise his own syllabus, be his own examiner. 'Judge the value of what I am doing by what you can see, by the promise I show . . . The bigger the building, the longer it takes to build.' His studies must continue until he had mas-tered every aspect of the natural sciences. The building he had in mind would be a landmark for all time.

The bemused 'Torf Inspektor' gave his blessing and young Ludwig soared still further beyond his orbit of understanding. Encouragement he now derived from the acquaintance of two young Englishmen, John and William Nicholson, who were also studying at Berlin and Göttingen. The elder brother was an oriental scholar, the younger an aspiring naturalist. Although both befriended Leichhardt and admired him, it was William, the younger, who became his patron and paid his keep once the aunt had died. After a joint foray with vascula and hammers in the Harz mountains, Leichhardt accompanied William to England and spent a happy summer botanising from the Nicholson home near Bristol.

The friendship was to last their lifetime. It offered mutual encouragement and a companionship which Leichhardt craved but rarely found. It was a meeting of minds and of youthful aspirations. But it was an unequal friendship. The Englishman provided, the German disposed. Nicholson was content to play Boswell to Leichhardt's Johnson. It was as if he was under the other's spell. And he considered the spell well worth as much as he could afford to invest in it.

For, in exchange for financial support, what Leichhardt had to offer William – and what he would one day be offering the wordy Russell in his cabin on the Condamine River – was the privilege of sharing in his dreams. Gauche and self-absorbed the young German may have been, but his enthusiasm for his work, and his vision of its purpose and outcome were truly intoxicating. 'The understanding of nature is what most interests me,' he tried to explain to his father. Everything in the natural world – be it the formation of peat or the passage of the sun – could be explained in terms of natural laws and, in the fashionable belief that an understanding of them would usher in a new era of prosperity, progress and peace, he saw the scientific pioneer as the hero of the age. Science made all things possible. It was as revolutionary as steam power and as exciting as alchemy. Chipping at fossils, dissecting fishes, and collecting flora, he saw himself as readjusting man's relationship with his surroundings. Academic study of such incalculable value would ensure his eventual celebrity, but the practical application of scientific methods in some new and unexplored theatre of the world offered the chance of even earlier acclaim.

In 1835, while still in Berlin, he had discussed with John Nicholson the idea of travelling in America. Two years later,

7 'The Pedestrian', Capt. John Dundas Cohrane R.N.
8 'The first native of Kamchatka that ever visited happy Britain'; Mrs
John Dundas Cochrane
9 'I entered Moscow at eight in the morning.' Cochrane had walked
the last 96 miles in 32 hours

Ludwig Leichhardt

LAURELS for Leichhardt! in Australia's name
    Evergreen laurels bind around his brow,
If Enterprise her guerdon still may claim
    Conquest and worth to crown, bestow them now;

10 'Doctor' Lugwig Leichhardt as portrayed by his admirer, James
Calvert
11 Journey's end. Port Essington as seen by Leichhardt in 1847
12 'The Blackfellows'. Charley and Harry Brown, trackers on the Port
Essington expedition.

13 'Doctor' Ludwig Leichhardt as portrayed by a critical member of his second expedition

in England, it was William Nicholson who was to accompany him and their destination was to be either America, North Africa, the East Indies, or – just possibly – Australia. Two more years of study and debate and at last the decision was made.

We considered circumstances, the position, climate of New Holland [i.e. Australia], its wealth in sea products, the anomalous character of its mammals; we reflected on its relationship to the bountiful archipelago which extends towards Asia on one side and America on the other. This was all discussed over and over again. The fascination of the unknown, the possibility of achieving something exceptional on a great scale, aroused our ambition. And so, instead of the safety of the West Indies, we formed and confirmed the resolution of seeking the fairer skies of Australia. There, if it please God, we shall follow our avocation and become 'interpretes naturae'.

By this time the two-man team of Leichhardt and Nicholson had transferred to Paris and, 'to plug other gaps', was studying human anatomy and geology. Leichhardt stalked the hospitals and morgues; to save his failing eyesight Nicholson took over the job of draughtsman. They ticked off their checklist of accomplishments. Soon they would be ready to take the field.

In the winter of 1841, by way of a trial run, they made a walking tour of Italy. Leichhardt did most of the walking while Nicholson preferred the extravagance of a ride. Both suffered from rheumatism and it was during a cold January convalescence in Naples that Nicholson dropped his bombshell: he had decided against Australia, against anywhere; he was going to Edinburgh to study medicine. Leichhardt was horrified. He felt betrayed. But 'I', he wrote, 'am not going to be seduced by the comfort of an English fireside'. He would go alone. He would leave within the year. And Nicholson, true to his word, would pay his passage.

During the same dismal halt in Naples Leichhardt received news of his father's death. He would have liked to have made a dash for Brandenburg, both to console the family and to say his farewells. But Prussia was now out of bounds to him. For years he had been trying to secure an exemption from national service. He had failed and was therefore, in effect, a draft dodger. In Prussia he would be arrested; only the sort of pardon that was occasionally granted to celebrities would enable him to return. It was another good, though unacknowledged, reason for forging ahead into the glorious future that awaited him.

That he, Ludwig Leichhardt, had been singled out for distinction he had never, through twenty-eight years of comparative obscurity, doubted. So certain was he of his glorious future that it was as if he lived his life backwards. He knew what he would become; the only challenge was to decide on the ways and means that would transform him into that reality. He had written his syllabus and chosen his field. Now, as pioneer, he had pin-pointed his arena. The great void that was the Australian Outback had, as he liked to put it, 'been allotted to me'. In his last letter before leaving Europe he anticipated the nature of his achievement.

Whilst the coasts of New Holland are slowly being populated, the nature of the interior remains entirely in the dark. Expeditions have been sent in, but they have made little more than short reconnoitring thrusts before either running short of provisions or being driven back by the hostility of the aborigines. The interior, the heart of this dark continent, is my goal and I will never relinquish the quest for it until I get there.

All that remained was to decide on the precise direction of his thrust and the means of organising it.

Sitting on Russell's verandah on the Darling Downs, Leichhardt listened to the talk of distant ranges and untravelled pastures. Out of the night came brave ideas and insistent voices that set him 'to overhauling the slack of his secret desires and aspirations'. Russell, the stockman, watched and prompted. At last the 'doctor' was 'brought up all standing by the strain of his own resolve'. The grand design, roped and hobbled, was ready to be led before his public. The decision was made.

It was about time. He had eventually sailed from Europe in October 1841. The passage aboard a ship crammed with emigrants had been uneventful but, to Leichhardt, immensely moving. 'I have crossed the vast waters of the deep and defied its storms,' he wrote to his brother-in-law. With only a needle to guide her and the wind to move her, the *Sir Edward Paget* had taken him half-way round the world. Was it not wonderful what nature and science could between them achieve? He had watched sharks and dolphins and albatrosses and learnt a bit about navigation. He had also acted as ship's doctor. Mustard plasters applied to all parts of the body had quelled a mild epidemic of scarlet fever but he had been less successful with sunstroke. This particularly affected the single young ladies who, in spite of his warnings, would parade on deck bare-headed, there to make advances to the young men. 'They were passing rapidly into hotter climes and must have been feeling the quickening of their natural impulses.' Fainting fits, then hysteria, were their only rewards. 'Two completely lost their reason and had not recovered it when we reached Sydney.' Leichhardt thought the root cause was boredom. Accordingly he started giving daily lectures on whatever seemed to be apposite – the clouds, the sea, the stars, or 'a review of the animal kingdom'. At first they were well attended. But as the ship dropped below the equator his audience deserted him. He put it down to a change in the weather. 'They gave me credit for good intentions . . . and left me in peace.'

After four and a half months at sea the *Sir Edward Paget* moored in Sydney harbour. Leichhardt leapt ashore as onto the Promised Land. 'With what delight did I greet every botanical novelty.' He felt so 'positively dizzy' with excitement that one wonders whether he too had sunstroke. Ships crowded the harbour and villas dotted the hills. Sydney was not the forlorn settlement he anticipated but a speculation-crazed city of 42,000. With expectations high and credentials at the ready, he set forth to offer his services.

But if Leichhardt was ready for Australia, Australia, though making rapid strides, was not quite ready for Leichhardt. In Europe his unorthodox education had proved a handicap; offers of his services had been shunned by the geographer Baron von Humboldt, by the botanist Sir William Hooker, and by London's Royal Geographical Society. But in Australia this same education represented something of an overkill. A list of savants whose lectures he had attended meant nothing to most Australians. They called him 'Doctor' because such a prodigious scholar must be a doctor of something. But while there were acres to be claimed, a colony to be run, and fortunes to be made, why should anyone trouble about scholarship? The pace of exploration was dictated by the need for more grazing, not by idle scientific inquiry.

Leichhardt waited on the Governor and presented his letters of introduction to the Surveyor-General, the instigator of all official expeditions. Neither took him very seriously. He cultivated the best society and ingratiated himself with all who showed a glimmer of curiosity about botany. Everyone was polite, some friendly, few interested. They seemed to shun his enthusiasm. 'I have often felt as if I were pretending to be the guardian of secrets, like the Masonic brethren . . .' He was learning not to declare himself lest he appear ridiculous.

Meanwhile a crisis was approaching. For the first time in his life he faced the very real possibility of having to find paid employment. William Nicholson had given him £200 to tide him over initial expenses. Eventually he found free board and lodging with a botanically inclined batchelor who was also Sydney's barracks-master. But somehow the £200 continued to evaporate. He delivered a few lectures at the school of Arts; they were poorly attended and unpaid. The donation of his minerals collection to the Sydney Museum also went unnoticed; the museum existed only on paper. Briefly he toyed with tutoring. His first set of pupils, all boys, were too easily distracted; his second, three sisters, were too much of a distraction. With one he fell moderately in love; that, of course, meant that he must resign as their tutor. But he had high hopes of being appointed superintendent of the Sydney Botanical Garden. The high hopes were quickly dashed; the job went to 'a mere gardener'.

Between these reverses he made exploratory forays around Sydney and began his study of Australian flora. In September 1842 he moved north to Newcastle to put his geological talents at the disposal of a local landowner and prospector, and to extend his botanical studies. He met his first naked aborigines (their lips were as large as horses', he noted, their penises unusually small). And he took his first uncertain steps into the bush.

It is difficult to find the way in the bush as the people in this part of the country are not careful in marking the trees . . . and as many great swamps exist here. Thus I lost my way a hundred times and I had only my compass to guide me.

On his next excursion the catalogue of disasters included setting fire to the hollow tree in which he was sleeping, being charged by a bull, losing his only pencil, and losing his horse (twice). The bull also accounted for the loss of his geological hammer. At its third attempt the brute contrived to trap him between its horns and a tree trunk. The 'doctor' retaliated by bashing it on the head with the hammer. 'Be it that this stunned him [he was writing in English for once] or was he tired, I managed – I know not how – to get from him and again behind a tree, trembling in consequence of the violent exertion over the whole body.' In the violent exertion he dropped the hammer; he did not return to look for it.

For a would-be explorer this was an unpromising start. Things could only get better. But whether he ever became adept in bushcraft is, like much else about Leichhardt, a highly contentious subject. His admirers credit him with a canny sense of self-preservation, a genius for reading the lie of the land, and the courage to live off its natural products just like the aborigines. He himself became convinced of his skills – and not without reason. But he would probably have credited them to science rather than instinct. For science, when applied to the matter of bushcraft, could outshine even experience. Once you understood the principles – geological, meteorological, biological etc. – of a country, you could go anywhere; then you were indeed master of its secrets. That was the beauty of science. It demonstrably repaid study.

But his critics saw it differently. Henry Stuart Russell, who would be one of them, was much amused to note that both the 'chimney-pot' and the 'cabbage tree', whose wearer was also short-sighted, appeared to have passed within a hundred yards of his shack without noticing it. By then Leichhardt's bush apprenticeship had lasted a full year as he made his way from ranch to ranch up the coast as far as Brisbane and eventually inland to the Darling Downs. He had learnt much and he had travelled far. But he still seemed severely handicapped as a potential explorer. How, quizzed Russell, could he possibly have missed the place?

'Well, I was looking all over the ground and up to the trees and through the air for what I could see, my friend. But I did not see your cottage.'

A preoccupation with the immediate foreground was no bad thing in a botanist. But his short sight also meant that he was incapable of shooting anything. He therefore never carried a gun and was never able to contribute to his larder. On the few occasions when a symbol of authority seemed called for, he preferred to strap on an old sword.

Equally disconcerting, to Russell's mind, was Leichhardt's attitude to the aborigines. Received opinion held that they were generally mischievous – the more so the further from areas of white settlement – and that the wisest policy towards them combined vigilance with bullets. Leichhardt rejected this utterly. He had joined an aboriginal gathering near Brisbane and had feasted with them on oysters, crabs and pine nuts; he had admired their agility and instincts in the wild; and he had observed their plight in the townships. Provided one's approaches were peaceable, he was convinced that they would not only respect the traveller but could materially assist him. Violence resulted only when white men appropriated aboriginal girls or when the aborigines acquired a taste for strong liquor.

Yet this was not to say that they could, or should, be left to their own devices. Caucasian peoples, he believed, were infinitely superior and, aided by syphilis and alcoholism, must soon undermine the black-fellow's existence. As always, Nature's laws – like the survival of the fittest – must be obeyed. The process was irreversible. But the white man might humour the black-fellow the better to study him; for he too had lessons for the scientific traveller.

Russell, hearing such sentiments, was not optimistic about his guest's prospects. He admired the gaunt German for his courage, his scholarship and his determination. He almost liked him. But as one of his neighbours remarked, "'tis my opinion that if Dr Leichhardt do it at all, 'twill be more by good luck than good management'. And Leichhardt needed both. For 'it' was 'the grand design', a journey into the interior, a marathon right across northern Australia 'from Moreton Bay to Port Essington' or, in a modern approximation, from Brisbane to Darwin.

The possibility of opening overland communications between the settlements on the New South Wales (and Queensland) coast and the solitary outpost of Port Essington at the continent's north-west extremity was nothing new. Amongst the Queensland 'squatters', like Russell, it had been busily canvassed for the past year. The *Sydney Morning Herald* had taken up the idea. And the Surveyor-General had led Leichhardt to believe that such an expedition was imminent and that he might be included on it. As usual it would be expected to blaze a trail 'in the wake of which', in Russell's inimitable prose, 'we pilgrim pioneers of pasture paradises might plant our portions'.

But labour, as much as land, was the cry of the moment. Recent legislation had ended the system whereby convicts were obliged to supply the colony's manpower needs. Suddenly hired hands were demanding at least £25 per year; profits were being halved; companies going out of business. Only a new source of cheap labour could restore the colony's prosperity; and there was no cheaper source of labour than India and South-East Asia.

Already it was known that Malay ships, mostly from Celebes (Sulawesi), visited New Guinea and the north coast of Australia. They came in search of pearls and an item of Chinese haute cuisine variously called *bêche-de-mer*, sea-slug, or sea-cucumber. Doubtless these piratical traders would also happily bring cargoes of indentured labourers once a demand was known to exist. So would ships from India and China. In return, wool, hides, and tallow could be exported. The sea lanes through the Indonesian archipelago to Timor, New Guinea, and Port Essington were already open. All that remained was to find a viable overland route south and west to Brisbane and Sydney.

First to benefit from such a scheme would be the 'squatters' on the Darling Downs. 'Squatters' was a misleading term; they were mostly high-spirited and well-educated young emigrants from Britain. Thus, when the Surveyor-General's expedition was suddenly postponed indefinitely, they were quick to revive the idea of a private initiative. Leichhardt just happened to be in the right place at the right time. At countless outposts he had listened and planned. Now, at Russell's, he at last declared himself. He, Ludwig Leichhardt, would shoulder the hopes and anxieties of the entire colony; he would lead an expedition himself. All he asked was for a handful of volunteers and for assistance with provisions. To canvass support and to despatch his collections he dashed back to Sydney. Five months later he was again on the Darling Downs poised, with men, horses, cattle, and supplies, for what Russell dubbed 'the doing of determined desire unto death'.

Russell himself was not one of the party. Leichhardt had understood that he and other experienced bushmen from the Downs would be joining him. But this was not Russell's understanding and already he was looking askance at the German's arrangements. The expedition included two aborigine trackers – which was reasonable – but the rest of the party lacked any relevant experience and can best be described as non-entities. James Calvert was nineteen and had been a steerage passenger on the *Sir Edward Paget*. So had John Murphy who was only sixteen and a hunchback. Of William Phillips nothing is known except that he was extraordinarily unsociable and a convict; he hoped for a pardon if he survived the journey. Then there was John Roper who may have been twenty but had only been in Australia for one year. Additionally an American negro and a local rancher started with the expedition but withdrew after a few weeks; officially they had volunteered to return in order to reduce the size of the party; unofficially they had fallen out with its leader.

And finally there was one last-minute recruit, a man of real experience who was probably in his thirties, knew Port Essington and its immediate neighbourhood, and who also had a scientific interest in the journey. This was John Gilbert. As collector of ornithological specimens for the distinguished London zoologist, John Gould, he had also travelled in Western Australia and New South Wales. In 1844 he just happened to be on the Darling Downs when Leichhardt was making his final arrangements. It was his own idea to enlist and he was remarkably frank about his reasons. They anticipate the prejudice which has bedevilled assessments of Leichhardt ever since.

When I first heard of the German's intentions I felt a little jealous of a foreigner being the first to make known the hidden treasures of this vast and interesting country which has been for so many years the particular province of my own countrymen.

National pride was at stake. But although the subsequent controversy concerning Ludwig Leichhardt's character and abilities would owe much to anti-German prejudice (fanned by two World Wars), it seems that in the 1840s Leichhardt's nationality carried no stigma. It was just a convenient pretext for, in Russell's case, ridiculing his pretensions and, in Gilbert's, gambling on them.

To Leichhardt himself it was, of course, cause for much self-congratulation. Here he was, the Torf Inspektor's son from Brandenburg, finally blazing a trail just as he had predicted.

If you recollect [he wrote to his brother-in-law] how ardently I used to look toward this unknown country you will appreciate the delight I feel now I am able to see and investigate the unknown interior. As I stride onward behind my long file of horses and companions I can hardly control my feelings. For I can tell myself 'This at last is the reward for your tenacity of purpose. You have managed to do what many a rich man neither could nor would do.'

The distance to Port Essington he reckoned at two thousand miles. Five to six months should do it and he was provisioned accordingly. 'When you next hear from me it will be either that I am lost or dead or that I have succeeded in passing through the interior to Port Essington.'

With a rousing rendition of 'God Save the Queen' (' a tune

which has inspired many a British soldier – aye, and many a Prussian too – with courage in the time of danger'), the expedition pulled away from the last squatter's camp on October 1, 1844. At first all went smoothly. The plan, in so far as such a thing was possible, was to hug the eastern slopes of the Great Dividing Range – thus running parallel to the Queensland coast – as far north as the Cape York peninsula, and then to cut across the peninsula's base to the southern shore of the Gulf of Carpentaria. On the seaward side of the range water proved plentiful and fine grazing was found along rivers which, after the expedition's benefactors, were named MacKenzie, Suttor, Burdekin. The only serious annoyance was the brickalow, a dense and prickly species of acacia which formed nigh impenetrable barriers across the bush and was already well known as one of the most formidable obstacles to Australian exploration. It took a fearful toll of clothes, packs, and patience; and Leichhardt seemed to have an uncanny knack of steering straight for it. It was also easy to get lost in. Horses, cattle and men periodically strayed and days were spent rounding them up. Soon it was apparent that Leichhardt's estimate of five to six months for the whole journey was wildly optimistic. Instead of fifteen miles a day they were seldom covering more than eight and were averaging rather less than four.

Accordingly rations of flour and tea were steadily reduced. The flour was eaten as 'damper', the chapati of the Outback. It was the bushman's staple and as stocks fell low Leichhardt's men grew anxious. They took to scraping from the ground the spillages caused by brickalow tearing the flour bags. 'Well mixed with dried leaves and dust' it was stirred into porridge, 'a mess which', according to Leichhardt, 'with the addition of some gelatine, every one of us enjoyed highly'. His companions were less enthusiastic about their leader's experimental soups and desperately sought to supplement their rations with game. Iguanas, opossums, emus, cranes, cockatoos and bandicoots (rats) were consigned to the stew pot. But true game, like kangaroos, ducks and fish, proved unexpectedly elusive.

In part the frustratingly slow progress was due to the cattle. At the suggestion of one of the squatters Leichhardt had made a last-minute decision to take sixteen bullocks. As a result the expedition was restricted to the grazing pace of a cattle drove. But they cost him little; like the horses, provisions and ammunition they had been willingly subscribed by supporters. And, as with many of the Doctor's unorthodox ploys, he had his reasons. People must understand that the scientific nature of his work precluded haste. Getting from one side of the continent to the other was less important than studying what lay in between. It might be possible to live off the country, but if not, the cattle were his insurance policy. For not only did they carry provisions but they also represented a considerable larder in their own right. To test this idea, a beast was slaughtered in early November. The meat, cut into strips, dried beautifully and, as part of a mixed diet, was most acceptable. Thereafter, as diminishing loads permitted and as poor hunting dictated, a bullock would be slaughtered every few weeks. Provided their systems could manage on a regimen which would eventually come to consist almost entirely of dried beef, they were practically self-sufficient. Leichhardt could feel justifiably proud of having solved a major logistical problem.

His companions, however, showed no gratitude. Chosen more with an eye to their compliance than their experience, they were proving a bitter disappointment. It may be in the nature of expeditions that the led complain and the leader ignores them; but Leichhardt's genius for antagonising his followers had all the makings of paranoia. The two aborigines he found totally untrustworthy; Roper he accused of impatience, irresponsibility and open defiance; young Murphy was foolish and easily led astray; not one of them could shoot straight; and Gilbert, the fellow naturalist and supposedly the most senior, took every opportunity to undermine his authority and evinced an intention of appropriating the results of the expedition.

In particular Gilbert enlisted one of the black-fellows to help him in making a rival collection of natural curiosities. At least that was how Leichhardt construed it. Gilbert was frankly amazed. He had been examining some rare snails found by the aborigine when the Doctor coolly appropriated them and told him to find his own. 'What may have been the cause of this conduct,' confided Gilbert in his diary, 'I suppose time alone will show; at present I have not the slightest idea.'

The puzzle was resolved on New Year's Eve, by which time they had covered about three hundred miles and were inland from the modern Rockhampton. Gilbert's attention had this time been called to the pods of some unusual legume. The Doctor was some way off but for once his eyesight did not fail him. 'For he came riding up very quickly and leapt off his horse and plucked the whole before I had dismounted.' It was typical of the man's jealous behaviour. 'Of course he did not offer me any.' Later the same day Roper killed a grey and yellow agama and presented it to Gilbert. Through Calvert, 'the Doctor's toady' and the only one who could do no wrong, news reached Leichhardt who promptly claimed the lizard as his own since it had been found by one of his party. Gilbert was advised in no uncertain terms that everything found by members of the party went into the official collection, that is, Leichhardt's. The only exception was birds; these Gilbert might collect 'because he [Leichhardt] does not understand them'.

Leichhardt was well within his rights. It was *his* expedition and it made sense to pool their findings. But that hardly excused his officious and dictatorial manner. He would lecture his followers but seldom confide in them. He expected subservience; he would settle for nothing less. Gratitude, it seemed, was not in the man. Increasingly they became aware of a single-mindedness, a preoccupation with his personal destiny, that seemed perilously close to madness. In January Gilbert calculated that, although less than a quarter of the way, they had eaten more than half their rations. Dissent was thus laced with fear. Twice Leichhardt went ahead to reconnoitre and got hopelessly lost. Were they too lost, going nowhere, merely acting out what Russell might have called 'a foreign fanatic's fantasy'?

Brush gave way to grassland, rock to verdure, massive gum trees drooped above a sea of brickalow. Then the brush returned, hemming them in; they strained to peer over it and saw more gum trees. The country was awesome not because it was inhospitable but because of its trackless, noiseless, and nameless emptiness. Lacking were any familiar bench-marks of progress. Each day was like another, each vista but a minor variation on an endlessly repetitive theme. They walked and rode as on a timeless treadmill, living from one new moon to the next and measuring their progress by the flow of a sluggish stream or by Leichhardt's latitudinal readings. In May, to the discomfort of the bullocks, they at last threaded the stony ravines of the Great Dividing Range; but the grain of the country continued to carry them north-west. (They were in fact north of Cairns and well up into the Cape York peninsula.) Leichhardt now attempted to establish their longitude, an altogether more difficult task and one which only Gilbert saw fit to record in his journal.

The result was anything but favourable being 141 degrees 25 minutes which in our present latitude would place us between 20 and 30 miles out to sea. The Doctor's certainty of depending on his observations must now give way to considerable doubt as to our actual situation on the map for former calculations may be equally wrong and thus every place we have marked down on the map may be incorrect.

Gilbert did not know whether to gloat or panic; and he did not have long for either.

A few days later a welcome change in the vegetation suggested that they must at last be nearing the coast of the Gulf of Carpentaria. They found a dead swordfish in a water-hole; it must have come up from the sea during a spate. Finally the two aborigines had an encounter with a creature 'about the size of a dog, trailing a long tail [and] making a deep noise like the bellowing of a bull'; obviously a crocodile, thought Leichhardt. The coast was at hand and, as usual, he was vindicated. On June 26 they turned south-west to follow the coastline round the Gulf. The plains were here intersected with lagoons and dotted with palm trees, a rich habitat for wallabies and ducks; for once they enjoyed a plentiful supply of game. But this natural bonanza had also attracted its traditional hunters.

Thus far, encounters with the aborigines had been few and brief. The black-fellows were curious about their white brethren but terrified of the monstrous quadrupeds with whom the white men appeared to cohabit. Indeed it was widely supposed that the aborigine of the bush, seeing only white *men* and seeing them forever leaping on horses, imagined that the quadrupeds were the females of the Caucasian species. Some such misunderstanding may have lain behind an apparently blatant attempt by the natives of the Gulf to round up and make off with the expedition's bullocks. The incident occurred on June 28 and was witnessed only by Leichhardt's two aboriginal trackers. Their shots, which dispersed the raiders, were heard by all, but their story seemed open to doubt. Gilbert and Phillips suspected that if the natives had attacked at all, it could only have been in retaliation. There were rumours, later confirmed, that Leichhardt's trackers had started the affray by surprising a group of aborigines and assaulting their womenfolk. The black-fellows had simply wanted to get their own back.

Leichhardt remained either unaware of these suspicions or deaf to them. On the evening of June 29, with 'smoke rising in every direction which showed how thickly the country was inhabited', he made camp beside a partially dried-up pool. The pool was screened by a belt of leafy trees amongst which the tents were pitched. It was the perfect place to be surprised in, commanding no view and impossible to defend. At about seven in the evening the men retired to their tents; Leichhardt and his two black-fellows fell asleep beside the fire. No watch was set; their guns were not even loaded.

The attack was almost over before they were aware of it. Missiles suddenly rained in on the tents and the trees erupted with warriors. Roper and Calvert were pin-cushioned with spears before they could even get out of their tent; then they were attacked with clubs. Murphy and Gilbert got out, and the former reached cover and returned fire. But Gilbert went down with a spear through the chest. In the open, Leichhardt and the two trackers scrabbled for firing caps and began to empty their guns into the trees. But already the attackers were melting back into the night. Their shrieks gave way to the groans of the wounded. Gilbert was dead; Roper and Calvert horribly wounded.

Mr Roper had received two or three spear wounds in the scalp of the head; one spear had passed through his left arm and another into his cheek below the jugal bone and injured the optic nerve, and another in his loins besides a heavy blow on the shoulder. Mr Calvert had received several severe blows from a waddi [club]; one on the nose which had crushed the nasal bones, one on the elbow and another on the back of his hand; besides which a barbed spear had entered his groin and another his knee. As may be readily imagined both suffered great pain and were scarcely able to move.

Leichhardt's experience in the Paris hospitals was now to be put to good use. Through the night he worked to extricate the barbed spears and staunch the bleeding. In the daylight he dressed the wounds again and then buried Gilbert's corpse. A second attack could be expected at any moment and must surely prove fatal. They could hear their assailants wailing nearby, apparently mourning their own casualties.

Through a second anxious night they watched and waited. The attack did not materialise and neither their cattle nor horses had been molested. Leichhardt resolved to move on.

In a case like this where the lives of the whole party were concerned it was out of the question to attend only to the feelings and wishes of the patients; I felt for their position to the fullest extent that it was possible for one to feel towards his fellow creatures so situated; but I had equal claims on my attention.

As usual, he was probably right. But feeling for the wounded was one thing; showing that feeling would have been quite another. Roper, for one, never forgave him for the agonies this decision to move on occasioned. It eclipsed any appreciation of the Doctor's surgical skills which had probably saved his life.

So determined was Leichhardt to put the incident behind them that in his narrative Gilbert's death is recorded without sentiment and mourned not at all. He could manage without the meddlesome ornithologist and made no secret of it. Yet he preserved Gilbert's diary. He must have known that it was highly critical of his leadership and might one day be used against him. But he was a man of honour and Gilbert had been a fellow scientist; destroying the diary would have been unthinkable. The priority now was to press ahead. If nothing else, the attack had served to remind him of their perilous position. Henceforth care was taken over the selection of camp sites and a night watch became standard. They covered fourteen and eighteen miles a day as they rounded the southern shore of the Gulf and headed towards Arnhem Land.

As the wounded recovered, their only thought was of journey's end. Flour, sugar, tea and salt were now exhausted. They lived off dried beef plus whatever the fit could forage washed down with Leichhardt's vegetable beverages. Half the bullocks were gone, ammunition was running short, and their clothes were no longer even decent. Any pretence of a shared purpose had also gone by the board. Leichhardt retired within himself, still mindful of his scientific responsibilities as he meticulously charted the transition from Australia's arid flora to a tropical lushness more typical of Asia, yet shunning company and preferring the solitary contemplation of his destiny. His men ignored him except to grumble at every delay. They performed their tasks mechanically; the only novelty they craved was survival.

On September 21, roughly a year after leaving the Darling Downs, they met aborigines who neither fought them nor fled. Some were covered in red paint and, curiously, all were circumcised. They appeared to be acquainted with guns and were anxious to exchange one of their women for a knife. Here at last was clear evidence that other strangers, probably from the Indonesian archipelago, had been this way before. It was a small but immensely reassuring discovery.

Thereafter the aborigines were increasingly friendly and even helpful. On their advice Leichhardt turned away from the Gulf up a river, christened the Roper, which promised to cut across Arnhem Land. Three horses were lost in a flood and they were down to one bullock as they at last emerged from the bush onto a rocky escarpment. There followed a steep descent into a new and humid land of swamps and crocodiles which Leichhardt reckoned to be the coastal plain. On November 26 they passed a creek in which the water was distinctly salty: he was right again. They were also visited by an aborigine who was wearing a shawl and cravat that were positively 'of English manufacture'. Excitement mounted. A week later another aborigine 'with the grace of an Apollo' accosted them with a speech in which they distinctly heard the phrases 'come here', 'very good', and 'what is your name?'. He could only have learnt them from the garrison at Port Essington.

Anyone who has at all identified themselves with my feelings throughout this trying journey, or imagined a tithe of difficulties we have encountered, will readily imagine the startling effect which these, as it were, magic words produced – we were electrified – our joy knew no limits and I was ready to embrace the black-fellow . . .

On December 17, 1845, after fifteen months that should have been five, the Leichhardt expedition straggled unannounced down a cart-track, past a few palm-thatched cottages and onto the parade ground that was the heart of Port Essington. A Union Jack fluttered from the flagpole and English voices greeted them. Leichhardt could hardly reply; the words kept 'growing big with tears and emotions'. He had kept his tryst with destiny. 'Tenacity of purpose' – sheer will-power in other words – had indeed been rewarded; science had triumphed.

More confident than ever that Providence, too, was on his side, he was unsurprised when within a month a ship happened to call at Port Essington, willingly risked a passage of the Torres Strait and landed the expedition, in late March 1846, safely in Sydney.

Here his arrival, again unannounced, caused a sensation. 'No king could have been received with greater gladness or deeper interest by the whole people than I was myself.'

As it had long been presumed that I had either died or been killed by the blacks, my good friend Mr Lynd [the barracks-master] had written my funeral dirge . . . My name was on everybody's lips for everybody was mourning for the poor unfortunate wanderer through the wilds of Australia; and none but a few went so far as to blame him for the foolhardiness of the venture. When nearly everybody had been affected by this prevailing mood of sympathy, sorrow and pity, I popped up out of my grave, successful in my undertaking and my pockets full of fine discoveries . . .

He could not have managed it better. Now they were penning paeans of rejoicing; there were balls and levees in his honour. People clamoured to hear his news or just to shake his hand. The government had voted him a gratuity of £1,000 and private individuals were busily raising their own subscriptions. 'The whole town is catching the excitement and going mad.'

For the Doctor's courage, determination and talents no praise could be too extravagant, but there were additional reasons for the excitement. Leichhardt was back; more to the point, his news was good. That pocketful of discoveries included inexhaustible pastures and benign, well-watered coastal plains. In the same year Charles Sturt returned from an epic journey into the interior. He nearly reached the centre of the continent but his tale was of terrible deserts and hostile tribes. Leichhardt, with only a little exaggeration, spoke of friendly natives and the enormous potential for ranching. It was what everyone wanted to hear.

He could also claim to be the first to have crossed the continent. A practicable route with water and grazing all the way had been traced from the east coast to the north-west. It might have commercial potential and it certainly had political and psychological significance. Thanks to Leichhardt, a vision was born of Australia as something more than a few coastal settlements linked by long sea voyages. Here was a pointer to the future, to a time when the continent would become a country and when its residents would turn their backs to the sea, open up internal communications and subscribe to an Australian consciousness.

The void of the interior was ready for the taking. Leichhardt's journey would inspire the south–north expeditions of MacDouall Stuart and of Burke and Wills in 1860. More immediately – and more ambitiously – it prompted his own follow-up. If there was one complaint about the Port Essington journey it was that he had kept too near the coast and done little to dispel the mystery of the interior. Now he would remedy that by crossing from the Darling Downs (or Brisbane) to the Swan River (or Perth). He reckoned it might take two and a half years but he planned to start in October; that was only six months after his return from Port Essington.

Hastily he prepared the narrative of his first journey. Written in repetitive diary form and packed with botanical and geological observations, it was never intended as an easy read for the general public. Heavy editing of both the style and content made it even more bland and impersonal. Leichhardt's readers would find him as cold and unendearing as had his companions – to whom, needless to say, he gave minimal credit.

How to find more suitable companions for the next journey was a pressing concern. Money was no longer a problem and bullocks were being pressed upon him from all sides. Men, too, were keen to nail their colours to his mast. But how would they stand up to the dried beef diet? And how could he be sure that they too would not 'resist' him? Interest in the success of the expedition must, he told one recruit, be matched by 'the perfect willingness to submit to everything that is required for that purpose'. 'Do never think of joining such an expedition if you find it difficult to obey . . . Believe me, for I have made a most disgusting experience!'

The recruit in question, Daniel Bunce, accepted these conditions. So presumably did the eight others who joined him on the Darling Downs in late 1846. Bunce was an experienced botanical collector and the rest, including a surveyor and a saddler, were all better qualified than his previous companions. 'I am expecting a very pleasant journey as regards personal relations,' he wrote. 'They are all young men, some of them very well educated and I have either known them for sometime myself or have accepted them on the best recommendations.'

With livestock comprising 40 bullocks, 270 goats, 90 sheep, 16 mules, 14 horses and 4 dogs it was a veritable farm that eventually struck west from the Darling Downs. Henry Stuart Russell again saw them off. He had reservations about the mules but with such a stampede of livestock the expedition could apparently survive indefinitely. 'I had great expectations of them,' wrote Russell, 'of bright days, bright deeds, and the brightness of a swoop upon the denizens of the Swan River.'

Russell was thus somewhat puzzled, eight months later, when one of his men reported seeing some of Leichhardt's mules heading home unattended. Had they simply escaped or had some dreadful disaster befallen the whole expedition?

A few days more – July 1847 – and back in funereal procession, wasted, woe-worn, wretched, wandered in, one behind the other, the hale, hearty, hopeful hands-in-hand who had gone forth so many weeks ago.

For once Russell had something to gloat about. The expedition had been an unmitigated disaster. Heavy rains had marooned them before they had even reached virgin territory and then a malarial fever had raged through the camp. Leichhardt ascribed it to too much fatty mutton. But when the remainder of the sheep and all the goats strayed and no one had the strength to pursue them, a change to beef brought no respite. In the moist atmosphere the meat, instead of drying, turned putrid.

Next it was the remaining bullocks who chose to escape. Leichhardt, feeling stronger, went after them. He recovered only four and when he got back to the sodden field-hospital that was his camp he found that the horses and mules had also taken off.

I now saw the thorough hopelessness of our position, that all further endeavour was vain, and that we had nothing for it but a speedy return. I cannot express the extreme agony of mind I endured when this distressing conviction came upon me.

Although a few of the beasts were subsequently recovered, most of the baggage, stores and ammunition had to be abandoned. The men were still sick when they straggled into Russell's station and Leichhardt himself was suffering from rheumatism so severe that he could scarcely climb on a horse. He was also experiencing another bout of paranoia. 'I made a serious blunder in the choice of my companions and I have been severely punished for it.' From the start the men had set out to undermine his authority; they were too soft for the task in hand, too mercenary, and too shallow; they failed to appreciate the gravity of the undertaking or to share his conviction of its importance; they complained about the lack of medicines; they gorged themselves on mutton; they laughed at his single-mindedness. Even after their safe return they continued to deride him and, unlike the non-entities of his first expedition, these were men of some influence.

But Leichhardt refused to give in. He would show them. The expedition had been aborted but the plan stood. He would start again as soon as he could re-equip and find a new team. 'My passion for the study of the environment here and my ambition to solve the riddles of this continent are boundless and beyond control.'

News of Europe's reaction to his first journey was at last percolating back to Australia. The Royal Geographical Society and its Paris equivalent had both awarded him gold medals. In Prussia von Humboldt himself was amongst those who had successfully petitioned for a pardon in respect of his evading conscription. The acclaim was timely. It stifled the whinings of his critics and it encouraged his supporters to back a new expedition. Naturally, too, he was gratified by such recognition. 'But whatever I have done has never been for honour. I have worked for the sake of science and for nothing else; and I shall continue to do so even if not a soul in the world pays any attention to me.'

A note of bitterness, even uncertainty, was creeping into his letters. The fiasco of his second expedition had revealed the possibility that Providence could be a fickle ally. Could it be that 'tenacity of purpose' could also fail him? Such unthinkable heresy made him even more determined. In March 1848 he was back on the Darling Downs with the Swan River again firmly in his sights. 'A strange change has come over my buoyant spirits of a year ago and I require the excitement attending a great enterprise to free me from fits of melancholia.'

During these fits of melancholia the bickerings of his

companions haunted his dreams. For a moment he actually questioned whether there might be something fundamentally wrong with his attitude towards his subordinates. But 'this depressing feeling of diffidence' did not last.

For after carefully thinking over the management of my expeditions and examining as impartially as I could the motives of my actions, I saw too clearly that under no circumstances I could and would act differently, as the principles on which I acted were the very essence of my individual character.

If 'tenacity of purpose' meant anything it meant pitting his resolve against all obstacles, human as well as natural. The laws of science allowed for no exceptions; neither would he. The disaster of the second expedition had served to show the 'unworthiness' of his companions. He saw it now as having been a necessary culling process.

The cull was radical; only one man, an aborigine, was retained. But in the newcomers he had, as usual, every confidence. They were mostly non-entities but they would do his bidding without demur. And this was more important than ever, for on this new expedition he expected to play a less active role. He was thirty-five; the hardships of the last five years were taking their toll. Gall-stones and diarrhoea on the first journey, rheumatism and fever on the second, had undermined a constitution never very robust. Latterly he had been 'suffering very greatly from palpitations of the heart'. He would be unable to handle the heavy chores, like loading the mules, and must reserve his energies for his scientific pursuits. More than ever he would be dependent on Providence and his companions. 'It [his health] is however by no means so bad that it might be considered a temptation of Providence in setting out on this journey', he wrote to an old friend.

You know well that I consider exploration of the continent my great task, which has been allotted to me and which my previous studies have rendered me capable of executing satisfactorily. I consider consequently the persevering in this line of my life my duty, even if my habits and inclinations allowed me to derive less pleasure from its pursuit than they actually do.

It was March 10, 1848 and he was writing from Russell's station beside the Condamine River. He told Russell that he would be 'out of sight' for at least two years, possibly three. They agreed to meet on his return and then parted amicably. On April 4 he wrote from the last sheep station on Fitzroy Downs. All was going well. He was 'full of hope that our Almighty Protector will allow me to bring my darling scheme to a successful termination' and he could not speak too highly of his new companions.

Then silence. Two years, three years, four years and still no sign of Leichhardt. Men, bullocks, horses and mules had simply disappeared into the Australian void.

In place of the man there grew the mystery; it too proved both controversial and intractable. For half a century explorers and prospectors would search for clues as to the party's fate. It was the completeness of their disappearance that was most puzzling. Not a stray mule, not a tattered shirt, nor a rusty gun was ever found. Trees with the L of Leichhardt scored in their bark were indeed reported, but so many and from every corner of the continent that they proved nothing.

Rumours abounded, some preposterous, some credible, none convincing. They simply stoked the fire of controversy. The disaffected companions of two expeditions made their feelings plain. Subsequently historians would pick over the diaries of Gilbert, Phillips and Bunce, the jottings of Roper and of the men of the second expedition, and the remarks of Russell. There emerged a comprehensive indictment of Leichhardt's leadership. He was inexperienced, inhuman, morose and selfish. If he owed his success more to good luck than good management he owed his failure more to bad management than bad luck. Evasion of military service made him a deserter; financial dependence on the likes of Nicholson made him a parasite; acceptance of the title of 'Doctor' made him a poseur. His achievement was fortuitous. His name should be struck from Australia's roll of honour.

But there were also Australians, particularly those of non-English extraction, who continued to remember him with admiration and even affection. They emphasised his courage, his vision, and his considerable scientific contributions. They saw his 'tenacity of purpose' as an essential qualification and his conduct towards his followers as no different from that of other single-minded explorers. There was even something romantic about his commitment to the Outback. They admired him too for all those qualities least evident in a thrusting colony – like indifference to money, devotion to scholarship, and concern for the indigenous people. They perceived his account of the first journey as a noble example of easy popularity being sacrificed for truth and science. Above all they wondered whether his reputation was not simply a victim of anti-German prejudice.

Australia was – and is – hopelessly divided about Leichhardt. There are 'Leichhardt men' and there are Leichhardt critics; there is no middle ground. All would concede, though, that he was, if nothing else, his own man.

CHAPTER FOUR
ODD JOBS FOR AFRICA
Mary Kingsley

The relationship between the traveller-writer and the lands he travels and writes about can be argued both ways; does the pen choose the place or does the place propel the pen? It may be, for instance, that the wastes of Siberia dictate a headlong style of travel and hence a fast and furious narrative. Had John Cochrane paused to discourse on whatever took his fancy, had he attempted colouring-in each sunset and polishing each paragraph, both journey and book would have overwhelmed him. Similarly Ludwig Leichhardt's prose, prickly, astringent and as unpalatable as brickalow, reads like a natural product of the Australian Outback.

But equally it could be that by some law of natural affinity the traveller and writer is drawn to the environment which most accurately reflects his, or her, own literary predilections. Such seems to be the case with Mary Kingsley. For a jungle of a book, maddeningly discursive but rich in reward, and for a profuse, riotous and equatorial style of prose, her *Travels in West Africa* overshadows all other productions. Like lianas her sentences loop and trail down the page defying the laws of grammar, subject and object lost to view, yet taking the reader unawares with florets of exquisite hue and always holding the promise, high in the tree cover or deep in the ground mulch, of some glimpsed creature of an entirely original imagination. Such a style is as obtrusive and ensnaring as the vegetation. So close is the affinity between author and subject matter that it is as if Africa was made for her.

But not Africa as a continent, be it understood (as she would say); just that particularly moist, malarial and mos-quito-ridden arc of it between Lagos and Luanda, what one might call the armpit of Africa but which she always called the West Coast. Initially 'I did not know the Coast and the Coast did not know me'. There were adjustments to be made by both parties; 'but we gradually educated one another'. A diligent pupil, she thought that she was the one to learn most under this arrangement. Others would claim that it was the Coast which reaped the benefits. Both are true. They were made for one another.

Even their faults they would learn to love. Amongst those of the Coast were mangrove swamps. As a collector of fishes Mary Kingsley got to know mangrove swamps well; and she wrote about them with many words and much feeling. Excepting the Congo (and a few others like the Amazon), 'all the really great rivers', she noted, 'come out to the sea with as much mystery as possible.' Shyly they prevaricate and recoil from contact with the ocean, preferring to yield their flood bit by bit to a host of sluggish arteries which themselves twist and fork before they fuse with the sea in an un-mappable tangle. So successfully did the Niger, the greatest of 'the really great rivers', surreptitiously unburden itself that for years its mouth was a greater mystery than its source, and even in the 1890s there was still some uncertainty as to which of the so-called Oil rivers belonged to it and which had their own watersheds. Between all these tangled arteries the land lay low and swampy. Here the tide was no respecter of coastline, and acres of mudbank, swamp and slime fringed each steely stream. This was the realm of the mangrove; and since most of West and Equatorial Africa's rivers drained to the west, most of the Coast was mangrove.

It was probably, she thought, the greatest swamp region in the world and in its gloom and size it possessed a grandeur equal to that of the Himalayas. She would refrain from calling it beautiful because 'its beauty is evidently not of a popular type'. But she found it so, especially when the tide had just turned. Then from the oily waters the long green-black stockades of mangrove foliage seemed slowly to rise up pulling their white roots after them. 'Displaying their ankles' she called it; and those aerial roots which depended from the topmost branches and forked in blunt fingers towards the mud were like hands trailed nonchalantly in the water. The mangroves continued to rise, their roots still bare and tangled, until at last they hauled the very mud from the bottom; and tide was out.

Some people thought the mangroves lifeless. On the contrary, according to Mary Kingsley they pulsated with life, although admittedly the quantity of fauna was not matched by a comparable variety of species. Mosquitoes, of course, abounded, and also flies 'particularly the big silent mangrove fly which lays an egg in you under the skin; the egg becomes a maggot and stays there until it feels fit to enter into external life'. There were 'slimy things that crawl with legs upon a slimy sea' and there were her own specialities, the mud-fish, cat-fish and a certain mollusc. And there were crocodiles. Everyone had crocodile stories and Mary Kingsley was no exception.

Now a crocodile drifting down in deep water, or lying asleep with its jaws open on a sand-bank in the sun, is a picturesque adornment to the landscape when you are on the deck of a steamer, and you can write home about it and frighten your relations on your behalf; but when you are away amongst the swamps in a small dug-out canoe, and that crocodile and his relations are awake – a thing he makes a point of being at flood tide because of fish coming along – and when he has got his foot upon his native heath – that is to say, his tail within holding reach of his native mud – he is highly interesting and you may not be able to write home about him – and you get frightened on your own behalf. For crocodiles can, and often do, in such places, grab at people in small canoes.

Low tide was only slightly safer. As the flood ebbed, waterways became trails of black and stinking slime and it was all too easy to find oneself trapped in their viscous puddles. Somewhere near Calabar, in just such a predicament, she had found a crocodile so bent on pressing his acquaintance that he climbed aboard. As his front paws came to rest on the stern of the canoe, Mary Kingsley moved to the bow; it was important to keep the balance right. She was also scared, although to say so seemed superfluous. The choice was now between gratifying posterity by jumping into the mud, there to sink, fossilise, and be unearthed a few millennia hence, or gratifying the crocodile by allaying his curiosity about the flavour of English limb. Happily Mary Kingsley was not so scared as to be resigned to either fate. She therefore grasped a paddle and 'fetched him a clip on the snout'. He withdrew; she paddled hard for deeper water. At times like this she wondered why she had ever come to West Africa and how anyone could be 'such a colossal ass' as to go fooling about in mangrove swamps. The crocodile did not return. In all honesty he was only about eight feet long. Many were twenty feet or more; he was just 'a pushing young creature who had not learnt manners'.

This encounter took place in the spring of 1895. At the time Mary Kingsley was thirty-two years old. She was on her second visit to West Africa and she was about to graduate from coastal swamps, the nursery slopes of African exploration, to the interior and the real thing. The crocodile, far from discouraging her, had actually increased her determination.

There are only two portraits of Miss Kingsley and both convey the impression of a severe and conventional Victorian spinster. In Africa as in London she habitually wore long skirts, high collars, cummerbunds and a small furry hat. All were black, stiff and forbidding. She parted her hair in the middle and coiled it tightly into an elongated and much pinned bun which was further squashed in place by the hat and its broad black ribbon which tied under her chin. Any resemblance to a Salvation Army chorister was incidental; but the result was equally unflattering, and, because she seldom wore anything else, equally distinctive.

It was, however, misleading. As a dutiful daughter and a reclusive blue-stocking she had adopted it as her uniform. But as a traveller, a dotty raconteur, and a controversial celebrity she would cling to it as a camouflage. In both incarnations she professed to spurn appearances yet the stiff crust of conformity could only be maintained by deliberate design and at some inconvenience. The same contradiction informed her whole life. Passion and enthusiasm for things, places and people had to be reconciled with starched and unshakeable ideas of duty, justice and patriotism.

Perhaps these two extremes were represented by her parents, her mother being a selfless, capable and daunting paragon while her father seems to have evaded his family duties to the extent of nearly forgetting he had any. Dr George Kingsley, brother of the novelist Charles (of *Water Babies* fame), spent most of each year wandering the globe as personal physician to rich, like-minded aristocrats. He shot and fished and pursued his esoteric inquiries into natural history and primitive religions. Home was where he dumped his books, hung his trophies, and told his stories. His temper, like his erudition, was formidable but often misdirected. There was probably as much relief as grief when the trunks were repacked for another long absence.

The home in question was a house and garden in Highgate, London. There Mary, the elder of two children, spent her first seventeen years, a closeted and self-contained child who made no friends and rarely ventured outside the gate. 'I knew nothing of play and such things', she later recalled and she evidently felt that she had missed little. But she was less resigned to being deprived of an education. Except for some German lessons her father seems either to have overlooked her schooling or to have deemed it unnecessary. She thought otherwise and took matters into her own hands. In the absence of teachers she worked her way along the shelves of her father's library. The fortune that was being spent on her brother's education resulted in a further influx of books; these too she devoured. But requests for more formal tuition were turned aside; 'my home authorities said I had no business to want to be taught such things, but presented me with a copy of Craik's *Pursuit of Knowledge under Difficulties*'. Seemingly her efforts were not taken very seriously.

No one would believe the number or character of the books I absorbed. I did not say anything about them, finding if I did, it generally meant an injunction not to do it. My favourites among them were Burton's *Anatomy of Melancholy*, Johnson's *Robberies and Murders of the Most Notorious Pirates* and Bayle's *Dictionary*.

In 1879 the family moved to Kent and her interests broadened. The world was still comfortably contained within high hedges and a rigid routine of domestic duties, but her bookish curiosity now ranged far and wide. She began organising her father's travel notes and researching for his projected opus on primitive religions. She also took up mathematics and science, the latter by way of a subscription to a periodical called *The English Mechanic*. 'What I should have done without its companionship between [the ages of] sixteen and twenty I do not care to think.' When one with hair as fair and straight as hers should have been passing long hours coaxing it into ringlets at the dressing-table, Mary Kingsley was practising her plumbing and experimenting with gunpowder and electricity.

Knowledge won in secrecy and against the odds was all the more precious and exciting. When, to be near her now undergraduate brother, the family moved to Cambridge, she eavesdropped on the world of scholarship and realised that she was not entirely a freak. As her mother's health declined and as her father lay up for ever longer spells of home leave, she added to the roles of daughter and nursemaid those of hostess and secretary. Visitors found Miss Kingsley demure, pale and painfully dutiful, but quite capable of holding her own in academic company.

Her only obvious failing, and one of which she was so aware that she rated it as an infirmity 'like being deaf or blind', was 'that I know nothing myself of love'. The confession was not especially painful. She had, of course, read about the thing and she had observed its workings in others. 'But I have never been in love, nor has anyone ever been in love with me.' Decidedly there were compensations. Subjects like natural history and mathematics – not to mention plumbing – which clearly bored others of her sex and age, she found fascinating. But why matters should be thus, why love did not interest her, she could not readily explain. The woman who emerges from her books is as warm and intriguing as the girl with the long fair hair sounds attractive. A square and flawless brow was, according to one contemporary, her chief beauty; others speak of blue eyes, a clear Nordic complexion, and a trim figure.

To Mary Kingsley the conventional image of the lady-traveller – rugged, manly, no-nonsense – is inapplicable. That rigid sense of duty, like the hairpins and the sombre dress, was designed to contain and efface a striking and wholly feminine personality. In her father and in her brother, and later in a host of West African merchants and sea-captains, she happily deferred to masculine qualities and would never aspire to them. She unashamedly claimed assistance as one of the supposedly weaker sex whenever it suited her purpose. And to the reader her narrative style, gossipy, profuse and hilarious, serves as a continuous reminder that he is travelling in the company of a lady. 'It's only me,' she was wont to say as she returned from the swamps or the jungle; and 'Only Me' duly became one of her West Coast nicknames. She would add the same dismissive rider after carefully arguing her point of view on some technicality of colonial administration. 'It's only me' meant 'it's only my idea', the idea of a closeted, self-taught, and now slightly travelled young lady. Not surprisingly she would show no sympathy for the suffragettes and would roundly condemn both their methods and their objective.

Whither such a dutiful daughter would transfer her devotion once home and parents needed her no more must have been hard to predict. No doubt she expected ample opportunity to consider her position and prepare herself. Perhaps one of her father's scholarly friends would take her on as amanuensis, even wife. Perhaps her brother would need a housekeeper and helpmate. Perhaps she would take up medicine. But in the end events happened so suddenly that they found her wholly unprepared. In February 1892, without warning, her father died; six weeks later her mother, whom for four years she had been nursing through an apparently interminable illness, abruptly followed him. Mary Kingsley found herself thirty years old, the possessor of a very modest income and, quite suddenly, beholden to no one. Yet within a few short months, and apparently without hesitation, she had adopted as the new object of her devotion and ministrations, the West Coast of Africa. It was as simple as that.

And then, when the fight was lost, and when there were no more odd jobs anyone wanted me to do at home, I, out of my life in books, found something to do that my father had cared for, something for which I had been taught German, so that I could do for him odd jobs in it.

It was the study of early religion and law, and for it I had to go to West Africa, and I went there, proceeding on the even tenor of my way, doing odd jobs and trying to understand things, pursuing knowledge under difficulties with unbroken devotion.

Elsewhere she records her curiosity, amounting to a hankering after the tropics. But Malaya was too far away and expensive, and South America too fever-ridden and forbidding. That left Africa. West Africa just happened to be the nearest bit. It was also a particularly promising area for one intent on doing 'odd jobs' for natural science and comparative religion; trading and missionary activity had as yet failed to penetrate any distance inland and she could therefore expect to find new species and unadulterated beliefs without having to mount a major expedition.

Immediately after her mother's death, by way of readjustment and recuperation, she treated herself to a trip to the Grand Canary. Apart from a week in Paris it was her first experience of foreign travel and, for a single lady in the 1890s, ambitious enough. Naturally she explored the island and inquired minutely into its trade and flora. The heat agreed with her and the light was so blue in the folds of the hills that she wanted to bottle some and release it back home in England; 'it would have come out as a fair blue violet cloud in the grey air of Cambridge'.

But what intrigued her most about the Grand Canary was its importance as a coaling station and infirmary for West Africa. Here for the first time she met representatives of the West Coast trading fraternity. A miscellaneous and much maligned collection of opportunists, scoundrels and romantics, they rarely survived long enough to enjoy the uncertain rewards of their work and were little better regarded than their slave-trading predecessors. Palm-oil and ivory were now the principal commodities and, whether manning the steamers of the West Coast shipping lines or managing some forlorn warehouse up a steamy equatorial creek, they were all lumped together as 'palm-oil ruffians'. But with their collective endeavours to survive, understand and regulate a corner of Africa Mary Kingsley would wholeheartedly identify.

To her they would become as dear and deserving as Africa itself.

Returning from the Canary Islands she and her brother bought a house in London. It was to be a base rather than a home. He soon left for Burma; she quickly read all she could about West Africa, sought advice on what to collect there in the way of natural history specimens, and in August 1893 sailed from Liverpool aboard a tramp steamer. To those, like the Captain, his crew, and just about every white man in Africa, who assumed that she must be a missionary or at least a roving representative of the World Women's Temperance Association, she declared her interests to be simply 'fish and fetish'. Fish – and beetles – represented her commission from the British Museum, her 'odd job' for its zoologist Dr Gunther. Fetish required a little more explanation. By it she meant Africa's indigenous beliefs and customs particularly in respect of spirits and taboos. It was her 'odd job' in memory of her father, an attempt to complement and complete his life's work on primitive religions.

Proceeding, like its unusual passenger, on the even tenor of its way, the ship called at the Canary Islands, Sierra Leone, and numerous ports along the coast, before landing her at Luanda, a Portuguese settlement and now the capital of Angola. Here she spent several weeks exploring and acclimatising and made a short overland journey to Ambriz. Then she headed back up the coast stopping briefly at Matadi on the Congo, Cabinda, Gabon, and Calabar. It was all by way of reconnaissance. At each stop she sized up the prospects for fish and fetish, made contact with the local traders and studied the terms of their trade. The last was important because in order to be able to travel inland she must pay her way and augment her resources by herself trading in piece goods and palm-oil. Currency was still practically unknown.

So, indeed, was administration. In 1893 the map of Africa was largely devoid of frontiers. Instead of bold lines running into the interior and meeting up with others, the only signs of territoriality were a few small and well-spaced nicks along the coastline. Located beside the mangrove swamps of principal

river estuaries, these imperial nibbles on the circumference of
the African cake were more trading posts than incipient
colonies. They flew the flags of a host of different nations –
Portuguese at Luanda and Cabinda, French at Gabon, Spanish at Rio Muni, German at Cameroon, and British at Calabar and the Oil River (Niger) ports; and in Europe their
respective governments were already chalking out tentative
spheres of influence in the interior. But on the Coast itself such
rivalry as existed was more often between competing trading
companies, competing missionary organisations, and competing traders and missionaries. An unattached traveller like
Mary Kingsley could move easily from one settlement to the
next without political complications. The fact that she was
also a woman, an unassuming but dedicated scientist and,
thanks to the *English Mechanic*, a most practical guest, ensured
a welcome wherever she chose to set foot.

By January 1894, after barely five months, she was back in
England with a respectable collection of fish, a few beetles,
and a commitment to Africa that now transcended mere
curiosity. 'I succumbed to the charm of the Coast . . . and I
saw more than enough during that voyage to make me
recognise that there was any amount of work for me worth
doing down there. So I warned the Coast that I was coming
back again . . .'

But it was not immediately possible. Her brother was also
home from his travels and, whether he wished it or not, and
regardless of her longing for Africa, duty demanded that she
keep house for him. That, however, did not preclude her from
making plans – plans in which there already featured a river of
peculiar interest, for it was 'the greatest strictly equatorial
river in the world' and 'the greatest river between the Niger
and the Congo'. It was called the Ogowe, it entered the sea in
what is now Gabon, and it was practically unknown in
Britain. But what commended it to Mary Kingsley's attention
was its combination of fast water, and so perhaps new fishes,
and the densest rain forest, home for 'a set of notoriously
savage tribes' including the cannibal Fan (or nowadays
Fang). The Ogowe River and the Fan tribes were to provide

the high point of her career as a scientist; she would be breaking new ground at last; and as a writer she would be stumbling on such a wealth of incident and novelty that even her profligate style would fail to squander the chance of a classic narrative.

Meanwhile she read, corresponded with fetish experts, and listened to Dr Gunther's ichthyological advice. At last, in true Kingsley fashion, her brother began packing. He was off to the East again – and she to Africa. She sailed from Liverpool in January 1895. This time the ship was a passenger steamer and she found herself persuaded into travelling, rather like her father, as the companion to a Lady MacDonald who was going out to join her husband, the Governor of the recently constituted Oil River Protectorate. It meant travelling in style and Mary Kingsley felt mildly compromised. She set more store by having become the proud recipient of a British Museum collector's outfit. Lady MacDonald, evidently intimidated by all the bottles and nets, tried to humour her companion by rhapsodising over every passing porpoise. She was unamused.

I used to look at them [the porpoises] and think it would be the death of me if I had to work like this . . . fearing all the while that she [Lady MacDonald] felt me unenthusiastic for not flying over into the ocean to secure such specimens.

Happily these early misunderstandings were soon overcome and they became the best of friends. After the usual calls at Sierra Leone, Cape Coast and Accra, Lady MacDonald offered her a base at Government House at Calabar which she readily accepted.

Before she could settle in, Sir Claude MacDonald was summoned on official business to the Spanish island of Fernando Po. Lady MacDonald went too and so did 'her honourary aide-de-camp'. Mary Kingsley had called briefly at Fernando Po on her first voyage. The island was both as beautiful and as unhealthy as she remembered. Luckily the Spanish Governor had removed his residence up into the hills and from there, in between official engagements, she contrived to slip away for some serious fetish hunting amongst the Bubis, Fernando Po's shy and little-studied natives.

The trouble with fetish and her other ethnological notes was that it was difficult to work them into a travel narrative. Some of this material she would hold back for subsequent publication; a lot of it was lumped together in five dense chapters bang in the middle of her narrative, and miscellaneous observations she simply threw in as she went along. This last was the fate of the Bubis; her distressed editor must surely have remonstrated, but for a characteristic apology.

I will therefore sketch the result of my observations [on the Bubis] here, doing so all the more readily because this book has no pretensions to being a connected work – a thing you have possibly already remarked.

In construction, as in style, *Travels in West Africa* has all the trackless inconvenience of the jungle. But, as she would write of the jungle, 'once you get used to it, what seemed at first to be an inextricable tangle ceases to be so'; 'a whole world grows up gradually out of the gloom before your eyes'. Hazards there still were; the unwary reader is liable to be suddenly tumbled into a tiger trap of machete-ed diary jottings, or tripped by some literary allusion lost on everyone except devotees of Johnson's *Robberies and Murders of the Most Notorious Pirates*. But in time one learns to recognise an anecdote in the offing, to enjoy the outrageous grammar as much as the outrageous humour that invariably brings it on, and to find one's own short cut round her rambling diversions.

The Bubis, though ethnologically interesting, were just such a diversion; she would later extract them from her narrative and make them the subject of a separate monograph. Returning then to the mainland and Calabar, she stayed on with the MacDonalds and continued her fish and fetish researches during short excursions up the Oil rivers. It was while thus engaged that she waxed eloquent about mangrove swamps and became so closely acquainted with crocodiles.

Acquaintance of a very different sort awaited her on another excursion up-river to Okyon, an isolated missionary outpost presided over by the formidable Miss Mary Slessor. Mary Kingsley always called herself 'a Darwinist'; she was a Christian, of course, but by no means religious and profoundly critical of missionary activity in Africa. Mary Slessor, by contrast, was a Scottish Presbyterian and had already spent eighteen years doing good works in what is now Nigeria, much of that time on her own and amongst some of the area's most feared people. Now, at Okyon, she 'ruled as a veritable white chief'. But, more to the point, she had acquired a profound understanding of African languages and customs and, in spite of her vocation, had considerable respect for them. Late into the night the two women exchanged ideas, Mary Kingsley becoming overwhelmed by the courage and insight of the only other Victorian lady to leave her mark on West Africa.

If only all missionaries were 'the sort of man that Miss Slessor represents'. But she stood alone. Run-of-the-mill missionaries would have regarded her hard-won acceptance by the Africans as tantamount to apostasy. Such people, wrote Mary Kingsley, saw African minds 'as so many jugs which have only to be emptied and refilled with the missionary's doctrine'. They totally ignored the fact that in African fetish, as in all religions, there were loyalties, constraints and attitudes that must be respected; or, if Christianity was the objective, at least accommodated. But the missionaries, to explain away their failure to make mass conversions, actually went out of their way to exaggerate the African's supposed failings, like cannibalism, polygamy, and drunkenness.

Mary Kingsley's views did not prejudice her appreciation of the kindness invariably shown to her personally by the different missions. It was just that as a white in Africa at a time of great political change it was inevitable that she should form opinions on the ideal nature of Anglo-African relations. And having gradually acquired some understanding of the problem, she was convinced that the interests of both Africa and the British empire could be better served in that climate of peaceful co-existence beloved by traders and planters than in the sort of confrontations to which missionary activity gave rise. Trade, and hence development and prosperity, flourished when the white man respected African tradition and discouraged tribal warfare. But tribal rivalries were actually exploited by the missionaries just as local fetish was flaunted. 'It's only me', she would add at the end of her outburst but such modesty could do nothing to diminish the highly controversial nature of such views.

As typical of an honourable and constructive trading company she would cite Messrs Hatton and Cookson. Liverpool-based, this house had been trading in West Africa for most of the century. But by the 1890s its operations in areas of British influence were being gradually incorporated within embryonic colonial administrations like the Oil River Protectorate. Its principal establishment was now therefore on French territory at Libreville on the Gabon estuary, a fact of considerable interest to Mary Kingsley in 1895. For the next river below Libreville was the Ogowe and, apart from a German company, Hatton and Cookson had a near monopoly of its trade. On Mr Hudson, Hatton and Cookson's Agent-General in Libreville, rested all her hopes; it was therefore to Libreville that she sailed from Calabar in May of that year.

Libreville, like Freetown, its British namesake in Sierra Leone, had been founded as a home for emancipated black slaves. The trading community were located at the nearby port of Glass where she disembarked, up steps 'only fit for a hen', onto Hatton and Cookson's wharf. She was met by Mr Hudson's deputy and immediately escorted to the Customs House. This too was approached by 'a veritable hen-roost staircase' and indeed the whole shack resembled a poultry house.

The officer is having his siesta; but when aroused is courteous and kindly, but he incarcerates my revolver, giving me a feeling of iniquity for having had the thing. I am informed that if I pay 15s for a licence I may have it – provided I fire French ammunition out of it. This seems a heavy sum so I ask M Pichault, our mentor, what I may be allowed to shoot if I pay this. Will it make me free, as it were, of all the local shooting? May I daily shoot governors, heads of departments, and *sous officiers*? 'Decidedly not'; I may shoot 'hippo, elephants or crocodiles'. Now I have never tried shooting big game in Africa with a revolver and, as I don't intend to, I leave the thing in pawn. My collecting cases and spirit, the things which I expected to reduce me to a financial wreck by customs dues, are passed entirely free because they are for science. *Vive la France!*

Disarmed but otherwise delighted, she put up at Hatton and Cookson's residence and spent the next two weeks either 'puddling about the sea-shore' or pounding round the countryside behind the deputy on a Hatton and Cookson's tour of the locality. At last the elusive Mr Hudson appeared in person. He disembarked from a river steamer, announced that he was about to re-embark for the Ogowe, and happily offered her a passage. They sailed from Libreville on June 5.

During the first day they steamed down the coast, across the Equator, and into the mouth of the Ogowe. Next day mangrove swamps gave way to the most magnificent forest she had ever seen. The gigantic trees were hung with creepers which fell so straight and evenly, and were so heavily laden with blossom, that they were like eighty-foot bead curtains. Each bend in the broad brown river opened new vistas of extraordinary beauty. Villagers rushed to the banks; but not till Lambaréné, a hundred and thirty miles up river, did the steamer finally tie up.

Lambaréné, soon to become the location of Dr Albert Schweitzer's mission hospital, already boasted a school and church run by the Protestant *Mission Évangélique*. Mary Kingsley spoke not a word of French but Mme Jacot, the missionary's wife ('that heroic form of human being whose praise has never been adequately sung') had excellent English and welcomed a chance to practise it. Mary Kingsley moved in with the Jacots. How long she stayed there is uncertain; it was probably about a fortnight but at this juncture in her narrative dates quietly disappear. 'For it is one of my disastrous habits well known to my friends on the Coast that whenever I am happy, comfortable and content, I lose all knowledge of the date, the time of day, and my hairpins.'

The next stage up-river was made aboard 'a charming little stern wheel paddle steamer'. Her operators, the *Chargeurs Réunis*, called her the *Éclaireur*; a better idea of her capabilities and crew would be conveyed by recalling the *African Queen*.

Besides Mary Kingsley, there was the extremely argumenta-
tive captain, who followed his every statement with a challenging 'N'est ce pas?', and three suitably eccentric fellow
passengers. One, 'a French official', danced a Highland fling
(to what was surely a hymn tune) on the roof of her cabin and
committed further mischief by putting it about that she was
'an English officer in disguise', presumably bent on imperial
espionage. 'Wish to goodness I knew French,' she wrote in her
diary; either that or at least 'how to flirt with that French
official so as to dispel his illusion'.

Meanwhile the river narrowed, its banks rising into a steep
gorge and its waters forcing the *Éclaireur* to fight to make any
headway. A hundred miles above Lambaréné an apoplectic
burst on the ship's hooter announced Njole. This was as far as
a river steamer could go and also, give or take a few latitudinal
seconds, the point where the Ogowe intersected the Equator.
Upstream lay a series of fearsome rapids, as irresistible to the
traveller as to the keen ichthyologist. Mary Kingsley therefore
settled down with another endearing missionary couple and
cast about for canoes and sturdy paddlers.

The Njole authorities, acting perhaps on the suspicions of
'the French official', elected to interfere. It was her only brush
with the French administration which for the most part she
found admirable. The Njole men affected great concern for
her safety and an even greater concern that they might be held
responsible for it. Did Mademoiselle not realise that although
one woman had preceded her up the rapids she had been
accompanied by her husband and a small army? To go alone
was madness. Mary Kingsley replied that she had every
confidence in the Igalwa canoe men now being recruited for
her by the missionaries and that she would only go as far up
the rapids as science required. 'And as for the husband,' she
told them, 'neither the Royal Geographical Society in their
Hints to Travellers, nor Messrs Silver in their elaborate lists of
articles necessary for a traveller in tropical regions, make any
mention of husbands.' It was a spirited performance. The
authorities departed, shaking their heads over 'one bent on
self-destruction'.

Next day, sitting on her portmanteau in the bottom of a native canoe, with a trunk of trade goods for a back-rest, the Tricolor flying from a stick in the stern and the wildest mess of rocks and white water dead ahead, she began to think more kindly of Njole officialdom. It was just possible that their concern for her safety was genuine. 'Jump for bank, Sar,' yelled M'bo, the stroke, at each particularly testing cataract. But the banks were either moraines of debris or sheer walls of rock. Scrabbling on the slippery gneiss and wading through the shallows, she was then expected to hack a path through the forest while the canoe was dragged up to the next stretch of calmer water. So it went on, with occasional interruptions for whirlpools, duckings and so on, through a long, hot day and into a long, dark night. Exhausted and with their canoe firmly wedged on invisible rocks, crew and passenger finally forsook the stream, stumbled through the shallows, and climbed into the forest in search of a village. Trees kept detaching themselves from the dark and crashing into them. Roots thrust at their knees and sent them tumbling into manholes full of boulders. But there *was* a village. They could hear the drums and soon they could see the lights. The villagers 'were painted vermilion all over their nearly naked bodies and were dancing enthusiastically to the good old rump-a-tump-tump-tump tune'. They were having such a good time, they explained by way of apology, that they had failed to detect the approach of their visitors.

Although not Christianised like the Igalwas, the villagers, Adoomas, were not unfamiliar with white ways, having been entrusted by the French with keeping open overland communications between the Ogowe and the middle Congo. They knew whites liked to eat in peace and so tactfully withdrew when supper was served in a threadbare hut. The bench off which it was eaten was to be her bed. Before turning in, Mary Kingsley stole off into the forest. Privacy was somewhat precious on an expedition; and what with the moon rising and distant mountains looming out of a thin mist, while the river thundered below and the fireflies danced all around, it was an uncommonly lovely night.

Do not imagine it gave rise, in what I am pleased to call my mind, to those complicated poetical reflections natural beauty seems to bring out in other people's minds. It never works that way with me; I just lose all sense of human individuality, all memory of human life, with its grief and worry and doubt, and become part of the atmosphere. If I have a heaven, that will be mine, and I verily believe that if I were left alone long enough with such a scene as this . . . I should be found soul-less or dead; but I never have a chance of that.

Some years later she would confide to a friend that she had gone to Africa to die. Obviously she took enormous risks – with her health especially. Everyone who went to Africa did. She drank only boiled water, carried her own tinned food, and took her quinine regularly. But so did other whites and they still died in appalling numbers. Mortality was like 'them mosquitoes', ubiquitous, ravenous, and somehow ridiculous. But in Mary Kingsley's case it may not be fanciful to suggest that the death she so willingly embraced had more to do with her own psychological turmoil. What she sought was a release from the claims of others upon her; and because to evade these was to deny that sense of duty which she held so dear, it was also a kind of death, an acceptance of failure.

That night she slept little. It was midnight before she returned to the village and at four a.m. she fell off her bench and out of the hut. By six the Igalwas were getting ready to return to the river. Another day, perhaps several, of non-stop excitement followed. Each time the canoe grounded they took to the water to push it free. Wading such an impetuous flood in a long skirt must have been as dangerous as it was inconvenient. After one upset she found herself marooned on a pillar of rock still clutching the Tricolor. Then a head-on collision with a tree trunk threw the six Igalwas and their paddles in a sprawling heap on top of her; it was, she thought, a wonder how they ever managed to sort out all those jumbled arms and legs. She lost her pencil, and her notebook dissolved into a pulpy mess; but her collector's bottles were filling with fish, the river was lovelier than ever, and she was sublimely happy.

Descending the rapids proved even more exciting. Hair-breadth escapes came so thick and fast that, had she had another pencil, she would never have been able to keep up with them. But without a major mishap it was all over rather too quickly. At Njole the *Éclaireur* was urgently taking on wood for another trip down-river. Her surly captain had wagered to outpace an impertinent launch and, with many a challenging 'N'est ce pas?', he hustled Miss Kingsley aboard. In spite of heaving to for an epic struggle with an 'hippopotame', he won his bet and within twenty-four hours both *Éclaireur* and 'hippopotame' were bearing down on Lambaréné.

Again Mary Kingsley stayed with the kindly Jacots. Immensely proud of the fact that she could now handle a small canoe on her own, she busied herself paddling across the river in search of specimens and visiting Igalwa villages. In the Igalwas she recognised one of the 'superior' tribes. She found good social and economic reasons for their polygamy and she related their fetish to that of the Bantu whose sophisticated belief system she was one of the first to appreciate. Igalwa jurisprudence was no less elaborate. 'But it would be desecration to sketch it; it requires a massive monograph.' As an anthropologist her methods may have been those of her age, her observations unsystematised, and her presentation of them at the mercy of her genre; but the respect, even reverence, with which she handled her limited materials shows little racial bias and anticipates the more perceptive attitudes of later generations.

This was true not only of the 'superior' Igalwas but also of the 'notorious' Fans. The value judgements, incidentally, were not her own; they simply acknowledged those then prevalent amongst the whites on the West Coast. The Fans were 'notorious' because they lived away from the coast, shunned what we would now call Westernisation, and were therefore credited with being irredeemable cannibals and reprobates.

To find out for herself, on July 22, 1895 she finally left Lambaréné and the Ogowe River, heading north into rugged and unexplored country sparsely but solely inhabited by Fans. Her ultimate destination was the Rembwe River which was said to join the Gabon and would therefore conduct her to Libreville. The distance could not be great, perhaps two hundred miles; but at the rate of one major alarm per mile, it was fraught with danger. Initially the alarms were of a familiar caste. She was travelling by canoe with four eager paddlers who contrived to fall in with crocodiles, hippos, and sandbanks. Although still unarmed herself, the paddlers had guns aplenty but did not actually fire them; one just went off spontaneously, missed the crocodile, but deafened the passenger and slightly singed her cheek.

A paragraph later – say ten minutes – she had forgotten all about it. 'Most luxurious, pleasant, charming trip, this.' The men were singing in a minor key some melancholic boating song and swinging their paddles in perfect rhythm. To the traveller, as to the reader, it was immensely soothing. Then suddenly, out of the blue, a devastating Kingsley flurry.

Nearly lost with all hands. Sandbank palaver – only when we were going over the end of it, slipped sideways over its edge. River deep, bottom sand and mud. This information may be interesting to the geologist, but I hope I shall not be converted by circumstance into a human sounding apparatus again today.

Rarely does an author's prose so accurately reflect, in its abrupt and confused phrasing, what was clearly a mishap but of a very unclear nature.

On the evening of day two they emerged onto a lake which the men called Ncovi. Well-wooded islands dotted its glassy surface and the forest rose steeply from its shores. It was exceedingly beautiful, very quiet, and slightly eerie. 'I smell blood', said Singlet. (Her men she named after their clothing, if they had any; hence 'Singlet' and 'Grey Shirt'. The other two were 'Pagan' and 'Silence'.) They headed for a large village on one of the islands; it was a Fan village but Pagan had the name of a man there who supposedly owed him a favour. This was their only entrée to Fan society and all depended on the presence and disposition of Pagan's contact. Taking no chances, each man primed his gun and clambered ashore ready for action. They were confronted by an enormous surge of Fans, also armed not only with guns but with wedge-shaped knives which they were ostentatiously loosing from their sheaths. The crowd halted a few paces in front of them and seemed to be working themselves up into a state of ritual anger. 'It was touch and go for twenty of the longest minutes I have ever lived.' At last Pagan's friend made a grand entry dressed in leopard skins. Evidently he was the chief. 'Pagan went for him with a rush' blurting forth the story of their last meeting. The chief 'grunted feelingly'; the panic was over.

Mobbed by what seemed like the entire nation, Mary Kingsley was led through the village, past the decomposing remains of last week's half-eaten crocodile and what might once have been an elephant, to the best house in town. She was still unsure whether the Fans really were cannibals but, since her men were convinced of it, it seemed wise to keep the number of Fan porters she must here recruit to a bare (of course) minimum. 'One must diminish dead certainties to the level of sporting chances along here or one will never get on.' The Fans were supposed to kill their victims on the march, eat as much as they could there and then, and smoke the rest for future use. Since she had no desire 'to arrive at the Rembwe in a smoked condition' she settled for only three porters.

After another disturbed night, most of which she spent paddling round the lake in search of glow-worms and indulging in a surreptitious bath, the party left Ncovi in Indian file, with loads on their heads in the best Saunders of the River style. 'Path in the ordinary acceptance of the term there was none.' But the Fans were great walkers, bounding over fallen trees, wading through bogs, and forging through an atmosphere that was never less than 'semi-solid' with sweaty, swampy exhalations, all at terrific speed. Luckily they seemed to need frequent meal stops which gave the others a chance to close up. Then Mary Kingsley would flop down beside them and 'thus a certain sort of friendship arose between me and the Fans'. One in particular, who wore his loincloth 'scandalously short', always appropriated her empty tins and seemed particularly drawn to her. The feeling was mutual, for to 'the habits of a dustbin' he added 'the manners of a duke'. 'My dear Princess, would you favour me with a lucifer?' was a rough translation of the request which invariably accompanied his fumbles in his loincloth for his pipe. 'I used to say

"My dear Duke, charmed I'm sure" and give him one ready lit.'

A herd of elephants briefly detained them and bequeathed them clusters of large ticks, a family of gorillas gambolled across their tracks, the Duke killed a snake which they later had for supper, they found the scratch marks of a leopard – and this was all on the first day's march. It ended with a celebrated episode which found Mary Kingsley playing the part of the leopard by crashing into a cunningly concealed pit, fifteen feet deep and lined with spikes.

It is at times like these you realise the blessing of a good thick skirt. Had I paid heed to the advice of many people in England, who ought to have known better, and who did not do it themselves, and adopted masculine garments, I should have been spiked to the bone and done for. Whereas, save for a good many bruises, here I was with the fulness of my skirt tucked under me, sitting on nine ebony spikes some twelve inches long, in comparative comfort, howling lustily to be hauled out. The Duke came along first and looked down at me ... 'You kill?' says he. 'Not much,' say I, 'get a bush-rope and haul me out.' 'No fit,' says he and sat down on a log.

The trap signified the proximity of people. Having extricated their employer, the Fans led her triumphantly into a surprisingly neat village. She was allocated a two-room house and was soon busy trading handkerchiefs and knives for balls of latex and elephant hair necklaces. For once there were no mosquitoes and she slept soundly. But in the early hours such a smell pervaded her apartments that she determined to track it down. It seemed to be coming from a small bag that hung, along with other talismans, from one of the roof joists. Untying it carefully, 'for these things are important', she emptied the contents into her hat.

They were a human hand, three big toes, four eyes, two ears, and other portions of the human frame. The hand was fresh, the others only so-so, and shrivelled.

So the Fans were cannibals after all. And how 'touching' that they should keep a little something of their victims by way of a memento. All things considered, she decided to forgo her usual night ramble and returned to her bench.

The next day and the following day, the fourth and fifth since leaving Lambaréné, they climbed what was in effect the watershed between the Ogowe and the Rembwe. It was not a well-defined ridge but a succession of very ill-defined ridges, cluttered with enormous fallen trees and cut about with landslides. In between the ridges was swamp which, where the sun could reach it, had a crust that could take the weight of a man but which, in the shade, took its revenge by sucking man, or woman, into sludge as deep as it pleased. As a result progress became slower, tempers quicker. Between the Fans and the canoe men rivalry gave way to hostility.

Mary Kingsley tried to arbitrate. In fact for the rest of the journey much of her time was taken up with what she called 'litigation'. Wherever they stopped, her Fans either provoked a new action by 'wife-palaver' or revived an old one by being recognised by a creditor. Nights not disturbed by raging hippopotami or marauding leopards, were rent by jealous husbands and officious bailiffs who would only release the miscreants after much negotiation and a hefty payment. For a student of native jurisprudence it was highly interesting; but she would have preferred to be an impartial observer.

Only slightly less harrowing than being a Fan magistrate was being a Fan doctor. In return for much new fetish data she made the mistake of agreeing to prescribe for her informant's wife. The lady in question was then fetched; she was not a pretty sight. 'The whole hand was a mass of yellow pus, streaked with sanies, large ulcers were burrowing into the forearm, while in the armpit was a big abscess.' After disinfecting the entire limb, the hesitant surgeon made a start with the abscess by cutting it open, whereupon the patient 'subsided'. Was she dying? Apparently not; she had simply fallen asleep. It was a case of spontaneous anaesthesia. Rumour that the white woman could guarantee a painless operation spread till the queue outside her surgery was like a doctor's nightmare. 'There was evidently a good stiff epidemic of yaws about; lots of cases of dum with various symptoms; ulcers of course galore; a man with a bit of a broken spear in an abscess in the thigh; one which I believe a professional enthusiast would call a "lovely case" of filaria, the entire white of one eye being full of active little worms and a ridge of surplus population migrating across the bridge of the nose into the other eye, under the skin, looking like the bridge of a pair of spectacles.'

Only her ever jaunty style betrays the fact that she was still enjoying herself – that and, once again, the disappearance from her narrative of all dates. Her wanderings in the Fan country certainly lasted four days and probably about a week.

At last, after a final extravaganza of chin-deep swamp from which she emerged with a fine collar of leeches, they struck the Rembwe and located a Hatton and Cookson's agent. In an end-of-term atmosphere she bought rum for the men and paid them off. They seemed highly satisfied and even a little regretful that the excitement was over. Her own sentiments were identical. But just when sobriety and reflection were in order, she was adopted by a bear-like Rembwe trader for whom she immediately conceived what, if she were anyone else, would have passed for a passion. His name was Obanjo – 'but he liked it pronounced Captain Johnson' – and his talk was as big as his frame. The booming voice and the back-slapping bonhomie suggested a born actor but underneath she sensed a roguish yet rock-solid companion. 'He struck me as being one of those men, of whom I know five, whom I could rely on.' His boat, in keeping with its skipper, was a roomy sea canoe of dashing lines but only half built and with a sail that looked like an old bedspread that had been patched with the Captain's cast-off dungarees. Across the stern was a bamboo platform which for three days became her roost. By choice she took the night watch, steering down the wide river with the Captain curled up at her feet.

He handed over charge to me as a matter of course and, as I prefer night to day in Africa, I enjoyed it. Indeed, much as I have enjoyed life in Africa, I do not think I ever enjoyed it to the full as I did on those nights dropping down the Rembwe. The great, black, winding river with a pathway in its midst of frosted silver where the moonlight struck it; on each side the ink-black mangrove walls and above them the band of star and moon-lit heavens that the walls of mangrove allowed one to see . . . . Ah me! give me a West African river and a canoe for sheer pleasure.

14   'It's only me.' Mary Kingsley in 1897. The hat is untypical

15

16

15 *Ctenopoma kingsleyæ*. Of two things Mary Kingsley was especially
proud: the Igalwa's approval of her canoeing and the British Museum's
approval of her collection of fish. This one was named after her
16 'A set of notoriously savage tribes.' Mary Kingsley was the first to
study the Fans, or Fangs, of Gabon
17 'A credible witness to remarkable experiences.' Louis de
Rougemont in 1898

18–20 De Rougemont's 'remarkable experiences' as faithfully portrayed by Pearce of the *Wide World Magazine*

18 Bruno and master spy their first visitors in two years

19 Having clothed Gladys and Blanche in cockatoo feathers, de Rougemont sets about boosting their morale with 'God Save the Queen'

20 'I then shot half a dozen arrows into the enemy's ranks.' Stilts and head-dress were as described by the white warlord himself.

19

20

Captain Johnson was so delighted with his mate that he proposed they extend the partnership indefinitely. She was tempted. Here was a man who made no claims upon her, and a life devoid of duty. She could dabble in trade and again go amongst the Fan and the Igalwa; he could finish the boat, perhaps build an awning over her bamboo platform and get a decent sail; he promised her 'plenty country, plenty people, elephants, leopards, gorillas'; there was a river in neighbouring Spanish territory which had everything: he would take her there. It was altogether the most exquisite of dreams and, weeks later, as she wrote up her narrative in sombre London, it seemed even more so. 'I am still thinking of taking that voyage', she sighed.

At Libreville the ever helpful but mildly disapproving Mr Hudson was waiting for her. So long as she was Hatton and Cookson's responsibility he would not let her out of his sight again. There was no need to remind her that she belonged behind mosquito-nets, that nights were for sleeping in, and that mud was not for wearing; she had never dispensed with long skirts and cummerbunds, nor ceased to be anything but a very Victorian young lady. But she had glimpsed another world and for this she was profoundly grateful.

To repay her debt to Africa now became her paramount obligation. From Libreville she sailed north to Cameroon where she began an ascent of Mungo Mah Lobeh, otherwise Mount Cameroon. It was pure indulgence. Neither fish nor 'good, rank fetish' were to be found on the cloud-wrapped slopes of the West Coast's highest mountain; even the chances of a clear view were slim. But, after four days of tough going, she stood on the rim of the summit crater and proudly recorded that she was probably the first woman and only the second Briton (the first was Sir Richard Burton) ever to do so. It was her way of memorialising her romance with Africa; and of saying goodbye. From Cameroon, in October 1895, she sailed for Liverpool.

At home her celebrity, even before the appearance of *Travels in West Africa*, was guaranteed. The newspapers clamoured for interviews, journals solicited articles, and a host of scientific

and charitable organisations requested her services as a lecturer. But when she obliged, the celebrity quickly turned to
notoriety. For in attempting to convince people that Africans
were not some inferior form of beings, she found herself forced
to make a spirited defence of cannibalism, witch-doctoring,
and even slavery – the very things which distorted ideas about
Africa and which she would therefore have liked to play down.

On the credit side, Dr Gunther at the British Museum was
decidedly complimentary about her collections. There was
one brand-new species of fish, six 'modifications of new forms
which have to have proper scientific names given to them', a
new snake, and eight new insects. For someone with no
scientific training it was a remarkable achievement and one of
which she was not a little proud.

Travels in West Africa eventually came out in 1897. Although
it ran to over seven hundred pages, about half of which were
devoted to fetish and trade, it enjoyed a modest success and
established its author as a humourist as well as a con-
troversialist. She could perhaps have done without these
labels but the idea was to draw attention to West Africa and
how better than by making her readers alternately laugh and
rage. For in the book, as in her articles and lectures, she
construed her role as that of lobbyist extraordinary for West
Africa. The scramble for Africa had now started in earnest
with the French laying claim to vast slices of the Sahel and of
the equatorial interior. Instead of responding the British
seemed content to sit on their existing possessions along the
coast which, in her view, consisted only of 'malaria, mud, and
mangroves'. Trade was what made them valuable but the
products on which that trade relied all came from the interior.
To protect her markets Britain must compete and push
inland. At a time when people were proud to call themselves
imperialists there was no prouder imperialist than Mary
Kingsley.

But this did not mean that she favoured colonisation. On
the contrary, she distrusted the Colonial Office, bitterly
opposed colonial administration, and thought the less
Englishmen in Africa the better. As against the missionaries,

so against the colonialists, all her sympathies lay with the traders. They alone could be guaranteed to interfere as little as possible with African society whilst inconspicuously promoting peace, prosperity and progress. In alliance with mercantile interests she argued for the minimum of indirect government over the maximum area.

But events were moving too fast, imperial prestige was too important, and trading companies had had their day. Africa's political future was being settled at the conference table, not in the boardroom. Mary Kingsley could, and did, influence attitudes to Africa, but she had little effect on policies. It was rather like nursing her mother during those last years in Cambridge, doing her duty to the utmost but knowing it was in a losing cause.

In March 1900 she set out for Africa again. Her intention, she announced, was to collect fish in the Orange River and then work her way back north up her beloved West Coast. But the Orange River was in South Africa and South Africa was now at war. Perhaps she was consciously reviving that unresolved psychological conflict and once again pitting her rigid sense of duty against her longing to be a mindless wanderer, 'part of the atmosphere'. The outcome was a foregone conclusion. As soon as she reached Cape Town she, literally, reported for duty.

She was assigned to nurse Boer prisoners of war at Simonstown. 'I never struck such a rocky bit of the valley of the Shadow of Death in all my days as at Palace Hospital, Simonstown,' she told a friend. Conditions were indescribable. In the overcrowded, bug-infested wards, tousle-headed Dutch boys were dying in their own filth of a virulent enteric fever. Another Florence Nightingale was needed and for a few weeks Mary Kingsley was just that. Then she too contracted the fever; she died on June 3, 1900. As a final gesture to the life she might have preferred to have lived, her last request was that she be buried at sea.

If it was indeed her wish to die in Africa it was granted. Simonstown was another of those 'odd jobs', another lost cause. 'The fact is,' she wrote in one of her last letters, 'I am no more a human being than a gust of wind is. I have never had a human individual life.' Her upbringing, what she called her 'religion', compelled her to live vicariously in the joys and sorrows of others. 'It never occurs to me that I have any right to do anything more than now and then sit and warm myself at the fires of real human beings.' She needed to be needed and was grateful for the odd jobs that came her way. But whereas once they had been her 'religion', after West Africa, after the Ogowe rapids and a week with the Fans and a few dreamy nights on the Rembwe, they were somehow less satisfying.

CHAPTER FIVE
'THE MOST AMAZING TALE A MAN EVER LIVED TO TELL'
Louis de Rougemont

'No one expects literature in a work of travel,' declared Mary Kingsley. She meant it by way of apology but, come the 1890s, it rang all too true. In the high summer of empire travellers flourished as never before; yet the fruits of their labours were growing pulpy and over-ripe beneath the sun that never set. Audiences, larger and less critical than their predecessors, rooted amongst these exotic windfalls and devoured whatever took their fancy. They liked their narratives tall and titillating. Adventures must be ever more stirring, lands ever more distant, peoples ever more primitive.

Catering to this market were not just books but, increasingly, magazines. Cheaper and more accessible, they ranged from the pacy patriotics of *The Boy's Own Paper* to the staid anecdote of *Blackwoods*. In 1898 the publishing empire of Sir George Newnes entered the lists with a middle-of-the-road monthly that cleverly combined the narrative appeal of conventional travelogue with the pictorial appeal of the *Illustrated London News*. Titled *The Wide World Magazine* (it later became the *Geographical Magazine*) it took as its motto 'Truth is Stranger than Fiction'; as if to prove the point, the more coloured a narrative the more lavishly it was authenticated with photographs.

Any story deficient in both illustrations and plausibility was unlikely to appeal to the *Wide World*'s editor. But as Edward Fitzgerald sat in his office on a summer's day in 1898 – and as he perhaps reminded himself of the first year's sales target – the revelations coming from his unexpected visitor began slowly to prime his curiosity. He weighed the man's modest and disarming manner against the inherent improbability of his story and decided that there might here be a case for making an exception.

His visitor, whose card announced him as a Monsieur Louis de Rougemont, had simply wandered in off the Strand. He understood, he said, that the *Wide World* published true stories of adventure and he was curious to know whether his own might be of interest. There were no pictures; the story was not even written down. But if he might be permitted, and if Fitzgerald had the time, he would tell it.

His English was slow but precise, his manner sober and diffident. Solemn, hooded eyes blinked apologies from a cracked and weathered complexion whence bristled a crop of short grey hair and an untrimmed goatee. He looked uncomfortable in a stiff collar; the crumpled tweed suit told of rented rooms and bachelor habits. Shrewdly Fitzgerald guessed that his story was also his meal ticket. 'I might have bought it for a £5 note; but I did not.' Instead he offered £10; it was by way of an advance. The crumpled suit accepted gratefully; a second meeting was arranged; and with the stenographer's transcript of the outline story in his pocket, Fitzgerald set off in search of corroboration.

Dr J. J. Scott-Keltie was Secretary of the Royal Geographical Society and Dr H. R. Mill its Librarian; they were also respectively President and Recorder of the Geographical Section of the British Association for the Advancement of Science. Two more eminent scrutineers could not have been found. In turn they perused de Rougemont's claims, consulted the relevant authorities, and finally pronounced. So authentic was the detail and so impossible its invention that they felt bound to accept the story as true; de Rougemont was indeed 'a credible witness to remarkable experiences'.

For Fitzgerald the news could not have been better. Suddenly he found himself sitting on the scoop of a lifetime. Sales would soar; the magazine was made. But he must protect his source and ensure that the *Wide World* had exclusive rights. At de Rougemont's next appointment a warmer reception awaited. A photographer was on hand to take the author's photo, an artist to sketch the main incidents of his story, and a battery of stenographers to record his every word. Several such sessions ensued, each more remarkable than the last, and by July the first instalment was in type. It appeared as the lead story in the August issue with an introductory note by Fitzgerald.

We now commence what may truly be described as the most amazing story a man ever lived to tell . . . Quite apart from the world-wide interest of M de Rougemont's narrative of adventure, it will be obvious that after thirty years' experience as a cannibal chief in the wilds of unexplored Australia his contributions to science will be simply above price.

Lest these claims should occasion some scepticism, Fitzgerald then quoted the verdicts of Mill and Scott-Keltie and announced that de Rougemont would himself be addressing the next congress of the British Association to be held in Bristol in a few weeks' time. Then he cleared the page to let the hero get on with his tale.

I was born in Paris in the year 1844. My father was a fairly prosperous man of business, a wholesale shoe merchant in fact; but when I was about ten years old my mother, in consequence of certain domestic differences, took me to live with her at Montreux where I was educated . . .

Skipping rapidly through his early years the narrator conducted his audience towards the scene of his adventures. In Switzerland he had learnt a little about geology and smelting, had enjoyed acrobatics and archery, and had resisted the demands from his father that he return to France to do his national service. Instead, 'to see what the experience of travel might do for me', he accepted 7,000 francs from his mother and set off for the East.

His ultimate destination was to have been French Indo-China; but in Singapore he got side-tracked. Peter Jensen, the skipper of a small Dutch schooner, was on the point of leaving for the pearl-fishing waters off the south coast of New Guinea. All he needed for this venture was a small injection of capital to make up the deposit against which he would hire divers. De Rougemont listened, then volunteered. In return for what was left of his 7,000 francs, he became a partner in the enterprise and the mate of the *Veielland*. They sailed for Batavia

(Djakarta), there took on stores and recruited divers, and continued down to New Guinea.

For pearling purposes Jensen and his divers left the schooner in de Rougemont's care as they quartered the shallows in a whale boat and numerous small skiffs. The mate's job was to open the oysters they brought back and collect up the pearls. Lest his readers should not be familiar with pearling he gave a credible account of the diving operations and a less credible account of their perils. These included giant octopuses which might entangle a man or even a boat with their tentacles, a monstrous fish 'with an enormous hairy head and fierce, fantastic moustaches', sharks of course, and hostile natives. After a short engagement with a flotilla of Papuan war canoes, Jensen moved to quieter but uncharted waters and diving operations resumed.

The hold was almost full of oyster shells and they had amassed some £50,000 worth of pearls when one day de Rougemont opened a shell containing three black pearls. Recalling that day he paused in his narrative, at a loss for words and overcome with emotion. 'Ah those terrible three black pearls; would to God they had never been found!' Black pearls were not just rare but priceless; a man could live comfortably for the rest of his life on the proceeds from just one. But Jensen was convinced that where there were three there must be more. Hence he insisted that they prolong operations long after a change in the monsoon winds heralded the end of the pearling season. Inevitably they paid the price.

'And now I pass to that fatal day that made me an outcast from civilisation for so many weary years.' It was sometime in July 1864. As usual Jensen and the men had gone to the oyster banks leaving him alone on board except for the Captain's dog, by name Bruno. When the wind got up, the diving party were still visible about three miles ahead. But the storm – it was a cyclone – came on with tropical suddenness; the whaleboat, far from making any headway against it, was being blown before it. As de Rougemont frantically battened down the *Veielland*'s hatches and lashed himself to the mast, he watched his companions disappearing into the gloom never to be seen again. To this day he knew not whether they had survived.

The storm raged for a day and a night. It carried away the sails and the rigging, it swept the bulwarks and wheelhouse overboard, and with the last went all the charts and instruments. The hull survived intact but with no idea where he was and without so much as a compass, de Rougemont's plight was desperate. 'Imagine the situation if you can.' He was alone, lost and powerless in the infinity of the ocean. Or almost. Frantic whines from the Captain's cabin cut short his moping. Bruno was safe and the dog's delight at being allowed back on deck galvanised his companion. A spare sail was found and a makeshift rudder was contrived from two oars. They sailed west and then south-west. In an archipelago there was, he reasoned, always a fair chance of a landfall. Meanwhile the ship was well off for water and food, and Bruno was proving an invaluable companion. 'I conversed with him almost hourly and derived much encouragement and sympathy therefrom.'

On the thirteenth day his prayers were answered. He awoke to find a strong current bearing the ship towards an island from which quantities of smoke trailed across the horizon. It was not, evidently, one of the Malay islands and the fire-raisers, black, naked and distinctly hostile, were not Malays. As the ship was mysteriously sucked into a natural harbour and then hustled down a long and narrow waterway, the savages went for their weapons; and de Rougemont went below. In due course spears began to clatter aboard. They were barbed and accompanied by sticks which made a whirring sound. Boomerangs? Rightly he concluded that he had blundered into a bit of Australia.

But which bit? Subsequent study of the map suggested that the narrow waterway, from which he eventually emerged into open water, must have been the Apsley Strait between Bathurst and Melville Islands. A day's sailing southwards and he would have spied the young settlement of Darwin. But how was he to know? He had some notion that he might make Timor if he continued west. West he therefore steered until, fifteen monotonous days later, the ship ground into a reef.

The shock was so severe that I was thrown heavily on the deck. Bruno could make nothing whatever of it so he found relief in doleful howls.

A wave carried the vessel free – only to dash her more violently on another reef. This time she was definitely settling. He thought of making a raft but the water was rising too fast. It was now clear that the reefs comprised a semi-circle in the lee of which lay a calmer lagoon and a low sandbank. It was their only hope. Man and dog abandoned ship and struck out through the surf.

And now occurred an example, amazing even by de Rougemont's standards, of canine fidelity. For Bruno, finding his companion unable to swim against the backwash of the breakers, took a mouthful of his hair – 'which, I should have explained, was very long, never having been cut since my childhood' – and proceeded to tow him to safety. Getting the idea of things, de Rougemont freed himself and clamped his own teeth on Bruno's tail so that he might be towed astern. He was a remarkably strong and sagacious brute – an Australian dog – and he seemed to enjoy the task.

At length I found myself on my legs upon the beach. When I had recovered sufficiently to walk I made a hasty survey of the little island or sandbank on which I found myself. Thank God I did not realise at that moment that I would have to spend a soul-killing two and a half years on that desolate microscopical strip of sand. Had I done so I must have gone raving mad. It was an appalling dreary-looking spot without one single tree or bush growing upon it . . . barely a hundred yards in length, ten yards wide and only eight feet above sea-level at high tide. There was no sign of animal life but birds were plentiful enough, particularly pelicans. My tour of the island occupied perhaps ten minutes, and you may perhaps form some conception of my utter dismay on failing to come across any trace of fresh water.

Two and a half years on a waterless sand-bar – he had posed the ultimate survival test. For maximum effect Fitzgerald of the *Wide World Magazine* should have ended the first instalment there. But his readership would surely have protested that someone was pulling their leg. It was vital to establish de Rougemont's credibility; accordingly the story and its lively illustrations – the hero finding the black pearls, the hero being towed ashore by Bruno etc. – was allowed to run for another ten pages.

What saved him, of course, was the cargo of the *Veielland*. The ship had settled on the reef but had not immediately broken up. He swam back out to her, built a raft, and began to ferry ashore her considerable contents. There were casks of water – not enough for two years but enough to keep him going until he had designed his own system of conserving rain-water. There were drums of flour and quantities of dried and tinned food. There were a few bottles of rum and there were some tools. The guns were useless because all the powder was soaked but he rescued a tomahawk, a harpoon and his precious bow and arrow; 'with them I could always be certain of killing sea-fowl for food'.

Most fortuitous of all was the fact that in New Guinea Jensen had thought to take on board a large stock of 'a special kind of wood'. 'This wood possessed the peculiarity of smouldering for hours when once ignited without actually bursting into flame.' It was much used by the Papuans to preclude the need for flint or matches and, for the castaway who had taken two days to strike his first spark, it was just the thing. Thereafter he never allowed his fire to go out. During the day he burnt driftwood and at night he covered the embers with the New Guinea logs.

From the *Veielland* also came some sacks of grain and lentils which he used for seed. For seed boxes he filled the largest turtle shells he could find with sand and watered them with liquid manure in the form of turtle's blood. Fine crops resulted, the maize being especially prolific, and soon the island was cluttered with blood-spattered cradles of cultivation.

His ingenuity knew no bounds. He built a hut using oyster shells for bricks and a sand/guano mixture for mortar; the roof was thatched with maize stalks. Out of shark's skin he made a hammock; he designed a sundial and an abacus-like calendar. It was vital to keep busy.

The great thing was to ward off the dull agony, the killing depression, and manias generally. Fortunately I was of a very active disposition and, as a pastime, I took to gymnastics, even as I had at Montreux. I became a most proficient tumbler and acrobat, and could turn two or three somersaults on dashing down from the sloping roof of my hut; besides I became a splendid high jumper, with and without the pole.

Even then the solitude would have been unbearable without 'my Bruno'. To Bruno he chatted, sang, preached, shouted, philosophised, and recited. Never did a dog receive so much undivided attention and never did a dog respond so heartily. Bruno's spirits failed not and his interest never flagged. He seemed to understand every mood and word. Even when his master was filled with a religious mania – brought on by his only reading material being a French-English translation of the New Testament – the dog joined in the hymns, sat through the sermons, and cocked his head in appreciation of each theological nicety.

Time passed. In the seventh month of their exile a sail was seen on the horizon. It passed without noticing the forlorn little flagstaff or the gaunt, gesticulating figure beside it. To avoid a repetition of this crushing disappointment he resolved to build a dinghy from timbers and canvas saved from the schooner. In nine months he had cobbled together an ungainly and extremely heavy tub. It floated surprisingly well and could even be sailed. But in the excitement of the moment he had launched it on the lagoon side of the island. There it stayed with its skipper unwilling to risk trying to float it over the reef and unable to drag it back out of the water and relaunch it on the other side of the island. There was not even much fun to be had from it. For thrills and spills in the safety of the lagoon he much preferred to leap astride a turtle.

Away would swim the startled creature, mostly a foot or so below the surface. When he dived deeper I simply sat far back on the shell and then he was forced to come up. I steered my queer steeds in a curious way. When I wanted my turtle to turn to the left, I simply thrust my foot into his right eye, and vice-versa for the contrary direction. My two big toes placed simultaneously over both his optics caused a halt so abrupt as almost to unseat me.

A further six months slipped by. The island was visited by a flock of parrots, closely followed by an almighty storm. On the first day of returning calm Bruno was out early barking at the breakers. Suddenly he bounded into the hut, tail gyrating with excitement, and would not leave until his master came with him. Outside, it was scarcely light. They made their way through the corn plots to the seaward shore and peered towards a grey horizon. At last de Rougemont made out a shape, long and dark, bobbing about beyond the breakers. 'Then, I must confess, I began to share Bruno's excitement.' The shape bobbed nearer. It was not a log but a well-built catamaran. Nearer still and he could detect 'several human figures lying prostrate upon it'.

And there, with his readers captive on proverbial ten-terhooks, Fitzgerald ended the first instalment of de Rougemont's story. An 'Important Notice' advised that this serial 'of unique importance and interest' would run for several months. 'You would therefore do well to order sub-sequent copies in advance.'

Sure enough, the September issue of *Wide World Magazine* was another sell-out. Overnight de Rougemont had become an international celebrity. His likeness was being moulded at Madame Tussaud's waxworks; the book and translation rights of his story were selling world-wide; and his services as a lecturer were being sought throughout the kingdom.

But fame so immediate is not won without controversy. In particular there were signs of professional jealousy in pearling circles, where £50,000 represented an unprecedented haul, and rumblings of unease from master mariners who pooh-poohed the size of his octopuses and ridiculed the technical-ities of turtle dressage. These doubts eventually surfaced in a letter to the *Daily Chronicle* written by a man signing himself simply 'An Australian'; and they were echoed in a leader in that much respected paper. Next day it printed a letter from Fitzgerald which staunchly defended de Rougemont, offered £500 to anyone who could prove that his story was faked, and urged the *Chronicle* to organise a public debate between de Rougemont and the Australian. The *Chronicle* in effect backed off and a week later carried a letter from de Rougemont himself. He now admitted that £50,000 was the figure given him by Jensen himself (who could have been exaggerating) and that he had never tried riding a turtle in deep water.

However he adhered to the principles of turtle riding as set out in his narrative, and the very next day received vindication from an unimpeachable source. Admiral Moresby knew the area as well as anyone, had given his name to the capital of Papua-New Guinea, and had been in charge of the Torres Strait pearl fisheries in the 1870s. From his retirement in Hampshire he wrote a letter to the *Daily Chronicle*. 'Having had some experience in turtle catching' he could vouch that de Rougemont's exploits were perfectly feasible; indeed he well remembered one of his own midshipmen enjoying a ten-minute ride 'sometimes on the surface of the water and sometimes under'.

Three things are certain [continued the Admiral]. First the ability of a man to get on a sleeping turtle's back; second by sitting far back on its shell to keep it near the surface; third, to instantly stop its career by reducing it to blindness . . . I can quite well believe that that lonely man on his sandbank, with all his instincts preternaturally sharpened did actually ride and guide the turtle as he has stated.

Many might feel, the Admiral added, that his personal experience also qualified him to offer some general opinion on de Rougemont's adventures. So far then as the narrative in the *Wide World Magazine* went, he was happy to report that 'I can honestly say I believe in them'.

At the time of writing it seems likely that the Admiral had seen not only the August instalment but also that for September. If so, this was indeed a vote of confidence. For episode two of 'The Most Amazing Experiences a Man Ever Lived to Tell' more than lived up to its billing.

It will be remembered that de Rougemont had been left standing in the shallows waiting to receive his first visitors in two years. In the catamaran he found a man, a woman, and two boys, all of them black, naked, unconscious and apparently dying of thirst. He bore them to his hut and began to treat them with rum and quantities of water. First signs of recovery were when each in turn cringed in extreme terror. 'I fancy they all thought they had died and were now in the presence of the mysterious Great Spirit.' Food and constant attention gradually overcame this fear. They began to prod and stroke their saviour while cracking their joints and making strange guttural sounds which he took to be 'expressive of amazement'. But never, it seems, were they entirely convinced that the white man was as mere a mortal as they.

In particular Mr Yamba, for that was the man's name, continued to regard him with intense distrust. It was reciprocated.

He was a big, repulsive looking savage with a morose and sullen temper and although he never showed signs of open antagonism, yet I never trusted him for a moment ... It seems I unwittingly offended him and infringed the courtesy common amongst his people by declining to take advantage of a certain embarrassing offer which he made to me soon after his recovery.

Mrs Yamba, the 'embarrassing offer' in question, was a very different case. She quickly learnt to trust him and even to dote on him. Although no conventional beauty, her eager face and 'sparkling eyes' betrayed rare intelligence. Soon she had begun to pick up a few words of English, de Rougemont's second language, and to teach him a few aboriginal grunts. Thus he learnt of her native land from whence they had been blown by the storm, of their long thirsty sojourn drifting across the ocean, and of their anxiety to return ·to their homeland, an anxiety which even his acrobatics and the wondrous contrivances of his island could not diminish. More to the point, Mrs Yamba, 'that devoted and mysterious creature', knew the way. She pointed to a star and insisted that they had but to follow it.

Here at last was a chance of escape. Although Bruno was decidedly jealous of the new arrivals, his master found the boys and their mother such a source of entertainment and gratification that life on the island without them would now be unthinkable. He therefore decided to accompany them 'in the hope that this might form one of the stepping stones to civilisation and my own kind'. Together they somehow man-handled his tub-like dinghy across the island, relaunched her in the sea, and began collecting provisions. He reckoned the distance could be anything up to three hundred miles and therefore allowed water for three weeks plus food including three live turtles. Then they waited for a favourable wind.

The voyage was eventually made in May 1867. Mr Yamba curled up in the bottom of the boat stuffing himself with precious food and was no help to anyone. Bruno and the boys sat in the bow and Mrs Yamba snuggled beside de Rougemont at the tiller. 'Night and day we sailed steadily on.' On the fifth day they reached an island which, though uninhabited, came as a joyful revelation being covered with tropical forest. They landed, cooked a turtle, and then pressed on. Five days more and Mrs Yamba was shaking him by the arm and pointing. 'I leapt to my feet and a few minutes afterwards the mainland came hazily into view.'

At the time, of course, he had no idea where they were or whether it actually was the mainland. But subsequently he had become convinced that it must have been somewhere near Cambridge Gulf at the northern extremity of Western Australia. His island he never identified but on a good map, three hundred miles to the west of Cambridge Gulf, may be found a small semi-circular reef which shields an atoll marked as Sandy Island. However improbable de Rougemont's narrative, corroboration was never very far away.

Even a long exile amongst the aborigines – which in de Rougemont's case was just beginning – was not unheard of. Many a ship had been wrecked on Australia's inhospitable coasts and there had been nearly as many castaways re-emerging from the unknown parts of the continent as there had been pioneers disappearing into them. In 1823, for instance, three men had spent seven happy months as guests of the Queensland aborigines. And when in 1849 a Mrs Barbara Thompson had escaped after five less happy years of captivity amongst the natives of Prince of Wales Island near Cape York, James Morill, from Maldon in Essex, was just beginning his seventeen years of exile also in Queensland. The record was held by William Buckley who survived for thirty-two years in the deserts of South Australia. Much of what was known of aborigine culture and customs was derived from such sources and it was to this knowledge that de Rougemont was expected to make a priceless contribution.

At the insistence of his passengers the tub-like dinghy was first moored on a small off-shore island. Here the Yambas lit fires whose smoke signals were immediately answered from the mainland. Three canoes put out towards them. Recalling Mrs Yamba's innocent chatter about eating enemies, de Rougemont observed their approach with some anxiety. 'I was in the power of these people, I thought; they could tear me limb from limb, torture me, kill and eat me, if they so pleased; I was absolutely helpless.'

In the event the natives were more scared than the white man. Only after Mr Yamba's bragging assurances that although no ordinary mortal the stranger was reasonably harmless, would they approach and begin the ritual examination of his physique and pigmentation. A roast turtle helped to put everyone at their ease; and when de Rougemont turned a few somersaults the Australians applauded delightedly. He was rewarded with an intimate corroboree at which the natives danced but 'all I was required to do was to sit beating sticks together and contributing to the general uproar'. At midnight he fell asleep.

Next day, after crossing to the mainland, the whole performance was repeated but on a far grander scale. Tribes from miles around had received news of his coming and now lined the shore in a vast surging horde. His boat, his bow, his dog, his tomahawk, everything was minutely examined, even his loincloth – incongruously it was of 'crimson, Japanese silk'. Poor Bruno was given a hard time by the local mongrels but, like his master, he too soon established a certain authority. The Australians seemed to welcome them not just as strangers but also as talismans.

Meanwhile Mrs Yamba, practical as ever, built him a grass hut and busied herself over his menu. Opossum, kangaroo, rat and various kinds of fish he liked; snake, whether baked or broiled, he did not. It needed salt and with this his hosts were unacquainted. Mrs Yamba also tried him on 'worms' (probably wichity grubs) – 'grilled on hot stones and eaten several at a time like whitebait I found them most palatable' – and on eggs. The latter were an enormous success and thereafter nests from miles around were raided to satisfy the white man's strange passion.

Mrs Yamba's solicitude was simply marvellous; but it was not without guile. After a few weeks in his new surroundings de Rougemont was one day confronted by two magnificently daubed chiefs holding between them 'a young dusky maiden of pleasing appearance'. One of the chiefs handed the white man his waddi, a big knobbed club, and signified that he was to hit the girl on the head with it.

Now I confess I was struck with horror and dismay at my position for, recalling what Yamba had told me, I concluded that a cannibal feast was about to be given in my honour and that – worst horror of all – I might have to lead off with the first mouthful of that smiling girl. Of course they had brought the helpless victim to me, the distinguished stranger, to kill with my own hands. At that critical moment, however, I resolved to be absolutely firm, even if it cost me my life.

Playing for time he sat down which was the signal for a parley. A large crowd gathered to watch the fun. The chiefs looked displeased and the girl was no longer smiling. But they too sat. Then, clicking and gurgling in his best Aboriginal, de Rougemont explained his predicament: the Great Spirit had advised him personally that eating people or even killing them was wrong. This, he told the chiefs, was his message for them; and he therefore begged them to spare the girl. 'I was very much in earnest and waited with nervous trepidation to see the effect of my peroration.'

To his amazement the whole nation began to roll about and roar with laughter. He thought it a bad sign. But 'then came Mrs Yamba to the rescue'. 'Ah, noble and devoted creature'; the very mention of her name stirred every fibre of his being. Standing by his side she gently chided him: silly de Rougemont, the girl was not for eating but for mating; with the club he must just tap her; then she would be his, his to have or – dare she hope? – his to swop.

De Rougemont understood. What a gem was Mrs Yamba. He tapped the maiden with the waddi; she fell at his feet;

celebrations immediately commenced; and before the feast was over he had arranged an exchange of brides with Mr Yamba. At the time Mrs de Rougemont, or simply 'Yamba' as he now called her, was 'about thirty years old and already beginning to show signs of age'. But he could not live without her; and it was to her stamina and bushcraft that he would owe his survival over the next fifteen years.

Even marital bliss could not reconcile him to an indefinite exile from the civilised world. Throughout the months spent on Cambridge Gulf he daily scanned the horizon for shipping and debated the possibility of an overland journey. For any escape bid he would need some source of light but high-protein food and he therefore took up dugong hunting. In any other kind of sport – like emu coursing or wombat shooting – he was liable to be outshone by the natives with disastrous results for his prestige. But thanks to his harpoon he could excel in tackling slow-moving mammals. Besides dugong he also secured a baby whale, an achievement which, like the carcase, went down well enough with his hosts although not with the mother whale who retaliated by demolishing his dinghy. Boatless now, but with a useful stock of dried dugong, he finally determined on an overland journey.

He had been with the Cambridge Gulf aborigines for nearly two years. Before conducting his audience to pastures new and adventures even more improbable, he was anxious to give some picture of their life-style. In lurid detail he told of battles and cannibal orgies, of hunting and fishing techniques, of ballads and clans and medicines and magic. This material was unavoidably discursive and Fitzgerald therefore preferred to hold it over until the next instalment. Already in type, this would come out in October; but by then the details, and indeed the rest of his narrative, were already public property.

For in mid-September the British Association held its annual congress in Bristol. Mary Kingsley was to address its members on African property laws but Louis de Rougemont was the star attraction, and with interest now at fever pitch it was inevitable that the press would report proceedings in full. He was to give two papers, one ostensibly on his geographical discoveries, the other on his anthropological observations. In reality both consisted largely of a résumé of his adventures. For the first time the whole of his thirty-odd years in the Outback was available for scrutiny and, whilst there were many who were reassured by his sincere and plausible manner, there were others for whom the sheer weight of coincidence in his narrative now crushed whatever fragile credence they had been willing to concede.

Briefly, his first overland journey was a disaster. Accompanied by Yamba and Bruno he struck off to the east with some vague notion that this would bring them to the Queensland coast and the pearling stations on Cape York. In a desert of red sand they could find no water and he was reduced to licking the dew and drinking rat's blood. Finally he collapsed and, with Bruno 'looking into my face wistfully and occasionally licking my body with his poor parched tongue', he slipped into oblivion. As usual Yamba came to the rescue. She took his tomahawk and drew water from inside the trunk of a tree. It was, of course, the bottle tree, a species well known to most Australians but unheard of in the Cambridge Gulf region.

After the drought, the flood. Continuing east they were taken unawares by a wall of water rushing down a dried-up river bed. Such a phenomenon was not uncommon in the Outback and he rightly judged that the rain, now falling so heavily somewhere up-river, would soon be upon them. Yamba hastily constructed a bark canoe and they paddled out into the stream. The river sped east promising a fast passage to the coast which he assumed would be that of Queensland. However, he now knew that the river was the Roper, so named by Ludwig Leichhardt, and that it emptied not into the Pacific but into the Gulf of Carpentaria.

Rapids, cataracts and hairbreadth escapes eventually gave way to a broad expanse of flood water from which only the tops of trees protruded. In their branches they took refuge from a school of alligators who prowled round the canoe 'snapping their capacious jaws' and 'roaring like lions'. Then at last into the sea. Set on the idea of Cape York, they headed north. Along the coast they met aborigines who could speak some English and Malay fishermen curing *bêche-de-mer*. When the latter offered to land them in Timor, de Rougemont was overjoyed. Yamba, though, put her foot down; she would not go. Although she had been a little off colour of late, this obstinacy mystified her husband and deeply chagrined him. But there was no question where his duty lay. 'Even if civilisation had been only a mile away, I can truthfully say that I would not have gone a yard towards it without that devoted creature who had so often been my salvation.'

Yamba's uncharacteristic behaviour was soon explained. They visited the site of an abandoned English settlement – which he now knew to be Port Essington – and while picking raspberries in its overgrown gardens de Rougemont contracted malaria. In five years he had scarcely had a day's illness; now he paid the price. A high fever was punctuated by long bouts of delirium. For days on end he failed to recognise even the faithful Yamba – an oblivion which, under the circumstances, he would not repent.

For when I came round a little I noticed a great change in Yamba, and I asked her if anything had occurred to her during my illness. I then learnt something which will haunt me to my dying day. There is perhaps no more extraordinary instance of womanly devotion recorded in the annals of the human race. To my unspeakable horror Yamba quietly told me that she had recently given birth to a child which she had killed and eaten!

'A thing so ghastly and so horrible' called for some explanation. Aboriginal women, overburdened with children and chores, often elected to sacrifice one child the better to feed and care for its siblings. The difference here was simply that she had sacrificed the child to save its father.

There are things of course too sacred to be spoken about here, but I think it may be mentioned as an instance of wonderful devotion that as I lay raving in the delirium of fever, the heroic woman who attended me had given me her own breast as nourishment.

Under the circumstances he could not find it in him to reproach her and by mutual consent they let the matter rest.

But a curious sequel to Yamba's ministrations was that her thirty-year-old husband was now left in urgent need of weaning. Milk he must, and would, have. How providential, then, that they just happened to be in the one corner of unknown Australia where buffalo's milk was available. For in its day, the Port Essington garrison had imported domestic cattle some of which had escaped and gone wild. Leichhardt's party had killed one and now the de Rougemonts, in spite of his still being convalescent, successfully trapped a cow and, with two well-aimed arrows, blinded a bull. The bull was also destined to contribute to his recovery. He finished it off with his tomahawk, split it open, and then, 'to test the efficacy of a very popular native remedy for fever', climbed inside. 'Fairly burying myself in a deluge of warm blood and intestines' with just his head protruding, he settled down for a long sleep. Twenty-four hours later Yamba cut him free. He emerged as from the womb, caked in blood, stiff and hideous to behold but rejuvenated: 'I was absolutely cured – a new man, a giant of strength.'

After further recuperation they continued round the coast in search of a white man's settlement thought by Port Essington's natives to be still occupied and which he now knew to have been Darwin. They must have been very near it when, as so often in de Rougemont's narrative, a storm blew them off course and carried them way out to sea. Mercifully they were spared another long sojourn on Sandy Island; but by an equally cruel coincidence they were eventually washed ashore in Cambridge Gulf within a few miles of their starting point eighteen weary months before. 'I tell you, my heart nearly burst.' De Rougemont was beside himself; was there any other known instance of fate playing such a miserable trick?

The members of the British Association must have been inclined to think not. From the crowded auditorium nervous coughs and the creaking of chairs might have suggested unease in certain quarters. The Frenchman, however beguiling, was laying it on a bit thick. And there were still twenty years of his exile to be accounted for. Whatever next? Could one man conceivably claim any more in the way of adventures?

De Rougemont seemingly could. Before setting out on his next odyssey he was persuaded to lead the Cambridge Gulf natives in one of their incessant campaigns. 'C'est magnifique mais ce n'est pas la guerre' he quipped as he described how he bamboozled the enemy by striding into battle with his hair bouffant to a height of twenty-four inches, his body a swirling mass of tattoos, and his feet on stilts. Naturally the foe took one look and bolted. His masterly battle plan, which 'oddly enough followed the lines of a famous historic Swiss encounter of five or six centuries ago', was thus never put to the test.

In spite of such diversions, life amongst his adopted people soon grew monotonous. More in search of variety than escape he decided to take Yamba and Bruno on an excursion down the coast to the south-west. The trip was uneventful until, somewhere in the vicinity of King Sound, a native let slip the news that not far away there was a local chief who had two white wives. Believing the ladies to be Malays, de Rougemont was not surprised, but he thought that he might as well investigate.

It was Yamba who first discovered the awful truth. While her husband engaged the chief, a particularly repulsive giant, in a customary exchange of compliments, she scouted through the camp and reported back that the wives were indeed white, fifteen and eighteen years old, and very miserable; and they spoke the same language as de Rougemont.

I confess a thrill of horror passed over me as I realised that two doubtless tenderly raised English girls were in the clutches of this monster. Once I thought that I must have been dreaming, and that the memories of some old story-book were filling my mind with some fantastic delusion. For a moment I pictured to myself the feelings of their prosaic British relatives, could they only know what had become of their long lost loved ones – a fate more shocking and more fearful than any ever conceived by the writer of fiction.

Of course, as the public would appreciate, much about the fate of these poor girls must be suppressed 'for obvious reasons'. Suffice it to say that with the chief's reluctant permission he at last managed to see them. 'They were huddled together on the sandy ground, naked, covered with dirt, and locked in one another's arms.' It was a most pitiable sight and one made still worse by their terror on seeing de Rougemont; somehow he had forgotten that he too was naked. Mastering their mutual embarrassment the girls pleaded to be rescued and de Rougemont agreed to do his utmost.

But first they had to be clothed. With his trusty bow and arrow he decimated a flock of cockatoos whose skins Yamba then deftly sewed together with kangaroo gut. Draped in these feathery shifts the girls recovered their composure sufficiently to give a coherent account of themselves. The story of their shipwreck and capture he would in due course give in the *Wide World Magazine* (thus, incidentally, providing Pearse, the magazine's artist, with subject-matter unequalled since the rape of the Sabine women). But, in present company, de Rougemont glossed over the subject. He did eventually rescue the girls – having rather unfairly pulled a knife on their repulsive captor – and he then escorted them back to Cambridge Gulf.

There, for nearly three years, his home became something between a ménage à quatre and a finishing school. Yamba kept house and worked her fingers to the bone foraging for food while the girls, still wary of the natives, bent to more decorous pursuits like millinery, music and amateur dramatics. Their simple ways and their total dependence on de Rougemont so charmed him that he happily dedicated his energies to amusing them. He whittled away at bones to make them knives and forks and he knocked up a rustic dining suite. For their violin bows he sacrificed some of his own flowing hair. Nothing was too much trouble. What with swimming lessons in the morning, cricket, rounders or football in the afternoon, and in the evening a musical soirée, recitations from Byron and La Fontaine, or tales from Shakespeare (*The Tempest* was their favourite, presumably because the props were all to hand), time passed happily enough. For the reluctant 'cannibal chief' it was an idyllic interlude and, when it abruptly ended, whatever charm his 'Robinson Crusoe existence' possessed vanished forever.

He blamed himself for the disaster. He had spotted a ship off the coast and, instead of quietly paddling out to investigate, he had excitedly roused the whole camp and set off with the girls at the head of a veritable armada. Waving and shouting they converged on the unknown craft whose crew mistook their intentions and manned the guns. In the subsequent confusion de Rougemont was blown out of his canoe, Yamba followed him, and the girls simply disappeared, presumed drowned.

I could not realise my bereavement. It seemed too terrible and stunning that when God had provided me with these two charming companions, who were all in all to me every moment of my existence, as a consolation for the horrors I had gone through – it seemed impossible, I say, that they should be snatched from me just at the very moment when salvation seemed within our reach . . . This dreadful thing happened many years ago, but to this day, and till the day of my death, I feel sure I shall suffer agonies of grief and remorse for this terrible catastrophe.

In his overwrought state he turned even on his native friends. They were just savages after all. Here there was nothing to keep him. He did not belong. His home, with the rustic chairs and the girls' half-made hats, he could not bear to go near. Taking Bruno and Yamba he turned a tear-streaked face to the south and resolutely set forth to escape from the Outback or to die in the attempt.

The rest of his story, though covering some fifteen years, was quickly told. For most of the time they were wandering back and forth through the heart of the continent. Events and locations had become somewhat confused in his mind. He recalled strange plagues – of rats, snakes, locusts, and even fish which fell with the rains and, as the water dried up, left the desert smelling like a canning factory. There were weird tribes, creeks rich in gold and deserts strewn with opals and rubies. They found a half-caste girl 'who I now believe to have been the daughter of Ludwig Leichhardt, the lost Australian explorer'; and for several months they cared for a deranged white man who, regaining his sanity just before he died, said that he was Alf Gibson, a member of the expedition led by Ernest Giles in 1873.

Bruno had become particularly attached to Gibson and was deeply affected by his death. A few weeks later the dog too died peacefully in his sleep; de Rougemont put it down to a combination of grief and advancing years. Yamba was also noticeably ageing. At some unspecified point in his story she had borne him two more children; they died young but, this time, of natural causes. Now it was Yamba's turn. In a most affecting scene he described her last farewells and her gentle passing. To say that he was distraught would be a wild understatement. But he was also released. As when the girls had drowned, he immediately turned his back on the scene and once again set forth with his resolve to escape fortified.

At last he was lucky. He stumbled on a prospectors' camp, stole some clothes, and was thus able to enter the next camp suitably dressed. Initially he was taken for a fellow prospector. But when he inquired what year it might be, explaining that he had been out of touch for a couple of decades, the men winked at one another and tapped their foreheads. As a harmless lunatic he was fed and directed back to Coolgardie and eventually Perth. There he had worked for a time at various odd jobs and then taken ship to Melbourne, Sydney, Brisbane and Auckland, whence in 1897 he had sailed to London.

So ended 'the most amazing story a man ever lived to tell'. Unquestionably it contained the seeds of its own indictment; but that was not quite the same thing as proving that all, or even part, of it was invention. Indeed, allowing for a generous margin of exaggeration, there were few details that could not be substantiated from other sources and few hard facts that could be openly contested. Leichhardt, for instance, could well have survived long enough to father a daughter; and if there were rumours that one of Leichhardt's companions had turned native and lingered on for years, why not Gibson? Certainly he had never reappeared. But what of the girls? Hard pressed on this point, de Rougemont eventually revealed their names. They were called Blanche and Gladys; their surname was Rogers. Their father had been the captain or owner of the ship whose wreck on the west Australian coast had begun their misfortunes. And the family came from Sunderland – or it might have been Newcastle.

Here were positive leads. Sleuths from the still sceptical *Daily Chronicle* were soon leafing through Lloyd's Register and making inquiries on Tyneside. But even after the British Association's congress de Rougemont seemed to be successfully weathering the storms of incredulity. Drs Mill and Scott-Keltie reaffirmed their belief that he was 'a credible witness'. Professor H. O. Forbes, although requesting further information on eighteen different points and although surprised that such a long sojourn with the Aborigines had produced so little new information, nevertheless had no doubt that de Rougemont's adventures were 'the result of Mr de Rougemont's own experiences in Australia'. Even the clicks and grunts with which he favoured Professor Tylor (Mary Kingsley's anthropological mentor) as specimens of aboriginal language were considered worthy of serious analysis.

On September 14 and again on September 16 de Rougemont submitted himself for cross-examination at the *Chronicle*'s offices and acquitted himself well. The editors of the *Chronicle* and the *Strand Magazine* found him 'a remarkable man' who clearly had spent much of his life 'under burning skies'. They thought his English a little too fluent and were not reassured by his insistence that he had learnt it at school, spoken it all the time with Jensen, and received further tuition from Blanche and Gladys.

On the other hand, we admit that he never seemed to be concocting a reply to questions which were sprung on him and his answers were singularly direct and explicit, and that it was clear that his natural intelligence and character were of a very high order.

The *Chronicle*'s claim still to keep an open mind more or less reflected the balance of letters for and against in its correspondence columns. There, Australians signing themselves 'Skewthorpe' and 'Sundowner' ventured vicious assaults from behind the safety of their aliases. There were, they claimed, neither emus nor kangaroos in the Cambridge Gulf region; it was quite impossible for a white man to live there so long or to travel so extensively without word of his existence reaching other white men; and how come he had passed right under the Overland Telegraph line without either mentioning it or attempting to follow it to civilisation?

A supporter responded by pointing out that the only journey that would certainly have taken him across the line of the telegraph was that to the Gulf of Carpentaria; that this had clearly taken place before 1870; but that the line was not completed until 1873. The case for the defence was made by men less concerned to conceal their identity and included academics, one of whom even verified the existence of giant octopuses, and Australian travellers. Many recalled the howls of derision which had greeted Du Chaillu's account of equatorial Africa and, in particular, its gorillas. Du Chaillu had been vindicated; so might de Rougemont.

Perhaps most exciting of all was a letter from a man who claimed to have met Peter Jensen. The pearler, it seemed, had not only survived that terrible cyclone but was now leading, in the wilds of New Guinea, a life as isolated and improbable as that of his one-time mate. Another scoop in the offing? The *Wide World Magazine* predicted as much and immediately announced its own expedition to find Jensen and secure his story. 'THINK OF THE MEETING BETWEEN LOUIS DE ROUGEMONT AND PETER JENSEN' screamed a massive headline in one of the largest advertisements the *Chronicle* had ever carried. 'THE MOST GIGANTIC SENSATION OF THE CENTURY' was about to have its sequel. 'The whole world waits breathlessly.'

It waited, in fact, for only three weeks. On October 7 the de Rougemont story was again hogging the headlines, thus edging out the Dreyfus case and a war scare in Africa arising from the Fashoda incident. But this time the papers were unequivocal and mightily self-righteous. '"DE ROUGEMONT"', 'THE BUBBLE BURSTS', 'Historic Imposture'.

Quite suddenly the loose ends of his narrative had all knitted together into an irrefutable and damning indictment. First to speak out was the Sydney *Daily Telegraph*. It identified a picture of de Rougemont in the *Wide World*'s first instalment as that of one Henry Louis Green, for seventeen years a resident of Sydney and now much sought after by the wife and children he had deserted. In France a noble family by the name of de Rougemont knew nothing of him and neither there nor in Switzerland were there any Greens. But there was, according to the *Daily Chronicle*'s stringer in the cantons, a Swiss family Grin. They were peasant farmers at Yverdon and they had had a son, Henri Louis, who had left home at the age of seventeen and never been seen again.

Finally, just prior to de Rougemont's first appearance in Fitzgerald's office, the papers had carried a report about a novel, but suicidal, deep-sea-diving apparatus which was being promoted by a Mr H. L. Green of Frith Street, Soho. In due course this report reached the attention of other marine engineers, two of whom had known Mr Green in Sydney. One tried to renew his acquaintance and was much amused to find that his old friend was now masquerading as de Rougemont; the other simply recognised his picture in the *Wide World*.

From these and still other sources the press pieced together the real story of Henri Louis Grin – or Green or de Rougemont. Leaving Switzerland he had come to England and somehow entered the employ of the actress Fanny Kemble as a footman-cum-courier. With her he had toured Europe. Next he had been employed as valet to a man who was then appointed Governor of Western Australia. It was as part of the Governor's entourage that he had met, and presumably greatly admired, a literary Frenchman by the name of de Rougemont. Shadowy years of odd-jobbing round Australasia followed. He was a waiter, salesman, cook on a pearling ship – which had indeed sunk – portrait painter and inventor of diving gear. Latterly, after deserting his wife in Sydney, he had made something of a name for himself as a spiritualist medium in Wellington, New Zealand. Thence to London where, after failing to interest anyone in his diving apparatus, he had taken to whiling away his time in the Reading Room of the British Museum. Works of travel took his fancy and thus were born the adventures of Louis de Rougemont.

By the time the storm burst he was enjoying a quiet vacation in Switzerland. The vacation was now prolonged indefinitely. He was last reported sitting in a café, alone and brooding. Truth, if not stranger than fiction, had run it a close second. But however bizarre his real story, it was not the one he had chosen to tell. And the telling was all. It was easy enough to scoff at the cold absurdity of it all in print; less easy to resist the charm, plausibility and inspired improvisation with which he had held his audiences captive. To his 'historic imposture' he had brought a flair and conviction rarely equalled even by bona fide travellers.

On June 9, 1921, in the infirmary of a London workhouse, 'Louis Redmond', alias de Rougemont, Grin, or Green, died. There was no obituary. But nine years later Sir Osbert Sitwell recalled with affection a tall bearded tramp who used to sell matches in Shaftesbury Avenue.

This ghost of the streets was dressed in an old ragged overcoat over the collar of which the thin hair fell and showed above it a calm, philosophical, curiously intelligent face.

He was repeatedly told that this man was de Rougemont. He could not vouch for it but with the reported death of Louis Redmond he noticed that the tramp was no more; thus 'this sad thoughtful spectre withdrew itself from the haunting of a busy world'.

CHAPTER SIX

'EVERYONE TRIED TO BE MY FRIEND'
A. Henry Savage Landor

In the autumn of 1898, when de Rougemont fever was at its height, another tale of improbable adventure was attracting the desultory fire of London's geographical savants. *In the Forbidden Land* by A. Henry Savage Landor, grandson of the poet Walter Savage Landor, was published by Heinemann in two massive leather-bound volumes and looked a very different proposition to the limp and frankly sensational pages of the *Wide World Magazine*. No expense had been spared. There were hundreds of photographs and drawings, some even in colour, and a large and business-like pull-out map 'based on the author's survey'. The spine was gold-blocked and the paper thick and glossy. It was a work, not a book; something for posterity to refer to and treasure.

But lest the casual reader should be discouraged by the evident weight of scholarship, a sub-title of more arresting intent had been added. 'An Account of a Journey in Tibet, Capture by the Tibetan Authorities, Imprisonment, Torture, and Ultimate Release' it read, and sure enough, in volume two, a succession of grizzly drawings depicted the author's terrible fate. Here he was, barefoot and bareheaded, being dragged behind a Tibetan pony with his arms tied and the noose of the tow-rope round his neck. Here was his faithful servant, described as 'the bravest man I have ever met in my vast experience of courageous men', being battered with knouts by two shaven-headed lamas and being incredibly brave. And here was the sinister saddle with the row of iron spikes by which the author had been impaled in 'the lower back' during a wild gallop on a much goaded steed. There were other instruments of torture, a vivid scene of the official executioner measuring his sword on the author's bared neck, and another, in mawkish colour, of the author being threatened with a red-hot branding iron. 'Bleeding all over – Insulted and spat upon – "Kill him!" – Urging on the executioner' read the chapter notes. They were echoed by the headings on each lurid page: 'Intense pain – Stretched and tied – Thirsting for blood – On the rack – The most terrible twenty-four hours of my life'.

Clearly Henry Savage Landor, who described himself as 'the artist and traveller' and whose previous works were listed as *Alone with the Hairy Ainu* and *Corea, or the Land of the Morning Calm*, had come badly unstuck in Tibet. Even when not chronicling the inhumanity of his captors his narrative was packed with tales of hardship on the high passes, of being hunted down by an army of two thousand men, of wading neck-deep through icy rivers, of falling three hundred feet down a mountain, and of living on a diet of nettle stew. The average gentle reader, never mind those whom he always called 'armchair experts', would find credulity under strain. But this was a possibility which he had anticipated. Most thoughtfully he had therefore arranged for his photograph to be taken and his wounds to be carefully logged immediately after his return to British Indian soil. Affidavits sworn by an American Baptist Missionary before a British official and attesting to every scar and scratch on his body were included in the book's appendices. Some of the 'wounds' could certainly be attributed to normal wear and tear at high altitudes; but there was no denying that he had also been mistreated.

It was also fairly obvious that he had asked for it. Taking to heart the words of Lord Salisbury about 'an Englishman's right to get his throat cut when and where he likes', Savage Landor had crossed from India into Tibet without either British or Tibetan permission. When turned back by the Tibetans he had promised to withdraw and then doubled back for the Tibetan interior. Contemptuous and trigger-happy, nothing short of brute strength and stout ropes could possibly have restrained him; and doubtless it was his oft-noted mixture of superhuman cool and withering disdain – which he called courage – that prompted his captors to try scaring him with instruments of torture.

That, however, was only half the problem. For, in spite of having spent most of his weeks in Tibet either in detention or on the run, Savage Landor insisted that his book was indeed of scientific merit and that advanced therein were some highly interesting claims. These were conveniently listed in the preface. They included: discovering the true sources of the Brahmaputra, Indus and Sutlej rivers and surveying those of the Ganges; proving that there was no connecting stream between the sacred lakes of Manasarowar and Rakas Tal (a highly contentious issue, this, since it affected the source of the Sutlej); climbing to a height of 22,000 feet without ice-axe, ropes, or even climbing boots (let alone oxygen); 'the fact that with only two men I was able to travel for so long in the most populated part of Tibet' (seven weeks to be precise, mostly spent in fear for his life); and 'last but not least, teaching non-Asiatic peoples to pronounce correctly the name of the greatest mountain range on earth, viz Himahlya and not Himalaya, a meaningless distortion of a poetic word'. He had also been the first European 'to enter the province of Lhasa' (though not Lhasa itself) and the first to have ascertained the height of the Trans-Himalaya, a range running north of and parallel to the Great Himalaya (or Himahlya).

In effect – and excluding Lhasa – he had as good as exhausted the exploring possibilities of southern Tibet. Or so he claimed.

But was he a surveyor? Well, no. Savage Landor had the costliest compasses, aneroids and thermometers but he was not a trained surveyor. He was an artist and as befitted an artist his map looked magnificent. But, as the infuriated geographers pointed out, it appeared to be little more than a rather good copy of the maps supplied to him by the Royal Geographical Society before he set forth. Then there was the matter of all those river sources. Given that he had never ventured far from tracks already travelled by other Europeans, it was hard to see how he could claim any new discoveries; even the rill that he named the Landor source of the Brahmaputra was not new. A few years later, in a nine-volume work on Tibet that includes what is still the most comprehensive chronicle of Tibetan exploration, Sven Hedin would dismiss Landor and 'his extraordinary Munchhausen romance' in a single paragraph.

A climber, then? A cragsman? No, once again and very definitely, according to the Alpine Journal. He claimed to have made his ascent to 22,000 feet from a starting altitude of 16,000 feet and at the end of a hard day's march. He dispensed with climbing equipment because he frankly despised it; it was cheating. And as if this were not handicap enough, he had insisted on carrying a pack stuffed with silver rupees and weighing 60 lbs. Yet in just six hours he had stormed up the mountain, arriving on the summit in bright moonlight at 11 p.m. and returning to base by 1 a.m. The horizontal distance alone was 18 miles – 'quite a record at such great altitudes' as he rightly surmised. In fact, too much of a record. It was simply impossible. Either his altitude was wrong or his watch; probably the former. Two years later, in Nepal, he would claim an even higher ascent, indeed a world record. But on that occasion careful investigation of his 23,000-foot peak would reveal it to be a mere 16,500 feet.

In short, A. Henry Savage Landor was given to exaggeration and deserved something of the treatment meted out to poor Louis de Rougemont. From those into whose particular fields of study he trespassed, he received it, though in suitably restrained language. Some even suggested that he might be giving British travellers in general a bad name. But the press never hounded him; on the contrary, the *Daily Mail* was actually sponsoring him. Publishers vied for his manuscripts and reputable organisations begged his services as a lecturer; the crowned heads of Europe seemed to be queueing up to shake his hand. Though long on heroics and short on verifiable facts, his tales caught precisely the pre-1914 mood of imperial euphoria. Not for Savage Landor any nonsense like wedding an aborigine woman or upholding cannibalism. Through thick and thin, long and tall, he could be counted on to uphold the dignity – to reinforce the prejudices – of his class and race. If, in Tibet, he had gone a little over the top, an indulgent public was prepared to excuse his extravagance; mild eccentricity was no fault in a gentleman and, unlike de Rougemont, Savage Landor was very much a gentleman. He was also, surely, the most persistent, active and unstoppable traveller of his day.

Born in 1867 in Florence where his father lived the suitably dilettante life of a poet's son, young Arnold Henry had shown early promise as an adventurer and a horror. Aged two he toppled backwards off a wall, like Humpty-Dumpty, and fell twenty feet. 'I was picked up insensible and badly bruised.' The blow had 'affected my head considerably'. Thereafter he was subject to momentary black-outs and was incapable of committing anything to memory, 'especially poetry and history', unless he could visualise it. Happily the handicap did not affect the recollection of his own history. Aged three nothing much happened except that he was catapulted from the family carriage into a ditch, but at four he invented a new method of tree climbing which entailed throwing a rope over a branch and clenching one end in his teeth while he hauled hand over hand on the other. 'Result – my eight front teeth were torn from their gums.' He picked them up and ran inside to show mummy.

Aged five he jumped into a bath of scalding water ('I became one blister from head to foot'), got his head stuck through the balcony railings ('a blacksmith was sent for'), and was discovered in the act of being beheaded by a play-fellow ('Come quickly and see me cutting off Henry's head' the little executioner had shouted as he wielded the razor-sharp sword). He also started school.

In a few months I could speak four languages fairly well – English, Italian, French and German – and was always the first of the class at everything except memorising . . . I never made friends with other boys, although everyone tried to be my friend. I developed more than ever an insatiable desire to draw. All my spare time, and even during lessons, I was continually drafting landscapes or else caricatures of teachers and other children. Although drawn in a childish fashion, they were remarkably like the originals.

It was surely with children like young Savage Landor in mind that Hilaire Belloc wrote his *Cautionary Verses* ('A. Henry

Savage Landor/nothing lacked except for candour . . .'). And it must also have been for such little monsters that Matthew Arnold invented the public school system. Had young Henry been bullied and teased – as he surely would have been – and had he observed the unfortunate impression made by other spoilt and conceited brats, he might well have emerged a very different, and perhaps a very decent, fellow. He might too have learnt about those good old English virtues of moderation and understatement which are so conspicuously lacking in his autobiography.

But it was not to be. 'In those days my father was not well off,' he explained. They lived 'on the best street in Florence' but the family fortune was tied up in works of art. The walls were literally lined with paintings 'including the works of Italian and Flemish old masters such as Botticelli, Paul Veronese, Rubens, Van Dyck, Carlo Dolce, Michael Angelo [and] Salvator Rosa'. Maturing in a second Uffizi, young Savage Landor continued to show promise as an artist yet was first sent to the local Technical Institute, there to study engineering and mathematics. 'How I got through my examinations so well was always a marvel to me.' But at last he had his way. He was enrolled as a pupil under the Irish portraitist, Harry Jones Thaddeus, and was allowed to give up the Technical Institute and spend all his time in Thaddeus's studios. There he drew people and, no less to his taste, there he met people.

Looking back in old age, the title he would choose for his autobiography was *Everywhere*; it signified the extent of his travels. But it could as well have been *Everybody* to signify the range of his acquaintances. As a dropper of names – personal names as well as place names – he knew no rival. His infancy had been disappointing in this respect; Garibaldi had hugged him and King Victor Emmanuel had given him a cheery wave, but that was all. Thaddeus's studios, swarming with visitors 'all tip-top people in the social world', offered a chance to make up lost ground. There he shook hands with Don Carlos, claimant to the Spanish throne, and with his daughter, the future Empress of Austria; he rubbed shoulders with the Duke of Mecklenburg-Schwerin; he played up to the Duke and Duchess of Teck, and he ogled the young Princess May, the future Queen Mary (wife of George V).

Naturally all these dignitaries were agog at his precocious artistic talent; but they were probably unaware that the fifteen-year-old was also a prodigious athlete, a versatile swimmer, a first-class gymnast, a keen cyclist, and a natural mountaineer. Copious incidents from this period bear out his prowess of which two are of particular significance. He had read somewhere that when a man was hanging from the gallows he 'experienced, just previous to dying, a delightful sensation'. Of course 'I did not believe it'; could anyone be so gullible? But just to show that his scepticism was well founded, he decided to give it a try.

It so happened that the Savage Landor residence included a gymnasium, fully equipped and no doubt lined with old masters. There, egged on by a companion who may well have been the same as the little fellow who botched the beheading, he tied a noose in a climbing rope and 'without thinking it over twice', shinned up a step-ladder, put the noose round his neck and jumped off. He was absolutely right; no delightful sensation. On the contrary. 'Beyond all expectation, my neck was being tightly squeezed.' The rope was unwinding itself, lowering and spinning him as it did so. And squeezing viciously. 'My face became highly congested.' His tongue was protruding and his eyes were about to pop out of their sockets. 'It was the most horrible sensation I had so far experienced.' It was, however, excellent training for being towed by the throat behind Tibetan ponies. At last he 'fell flat on the floor and was as ill as possible'. His neck was intact, ready once again to be stuck out whenever opportunity offered.

The sort of opportunity he had in mind was being much influenced by a book – it was, of course, a prize – about Samuel Baker's travels up the Nile.

I was simply entranced [he recalled]. Oh how I was longing to be a man and do like Sir Samuel, and go and see new countries and meet savages and wild beasts. Little did I think at that time that in the way of adventure I should have in later years enough to fill the lives of twenty men.

For the summer the family migrated up to the Apennines and here he first encountered the Italian Alpine Club. Armed with alpenstocks, axes and ropes some thirty climbers clumped round the village in hob-nailed boots and hats with feathers in them. They were about to make an ascent of a nearby mountain but when Savage Landor asked to tag along he was told to get lost. He resented this. At dead of night he stole from the house with a pocketful of biscuits and climbed steadily up the mountain. By sunrise he was on the top, fourteen miles from the village and several thousand feet above it. Eventually he heard the gallant alpinists tapping their way up below him. He lolled back on the rocks and pretended to read a newspaper. Puffing with exhaustion the Alpinists breasted the summit. How perfectly absurd they looked in 'such ridiculous costumes and carrying all that paraphernalia'.

They crowded round me and when they recognised that 'the mere boy and not even a member of the Alpine Club' had done with the utmost ease what they had accomplished with an almost superhuman effort, they felt rather small.

Thereafter he would cultivate a healthy disdain for anything in the way of specialised clothing or equipment. In the African jungle or on the Himalayan passes he would wear and carry nothing that would have disgraced him on the streets of London or Florence. Sun helmets and safari suits were as much anathema as climbing boots and parkas. It was all part of his travel philosophy. The idea was to yield not one jot, to make not one concession, to foreign parts or foreign peoples. Disguise was deceit, compromise cowardice. Travel he would come to see as a rather demanding game: the world was the board and the object was to get round more of its out-of-the-way places than anyone else. Camouflage automatically disqualified you, as did any sneaky little ruses like using ropes to climb mountains.

At the end, to prove that you had been there, you had to write a book and illustrate it convincingly. Documented proof was very important. In the case of Tibet it would necessitate those sworn affidavits and, in old age, it was the need to prove that he had indeed been 'everywhere' that would prompt the writing of his autobiography. Dropping names was a particularly useful form of authentication and during his early wanderings in more civilised parts people figured more prominently than places. Thus it emerges that at the age of seventeen he stayed with various relations in England and visited Windsor, where he met Algernon Swinburne, Warwick, where he met 'Charles Kingsley's daughter' (he probably means Mary, *George* Kingsley's daughter), and Cornwall, where he stayed with Sir Charles and Lady Graves-Sawle. With brushes and easel he walked round the coast of Cornwall and then enrolled in a famous atelier in Paris. Understandably the Parisian art world was soon abuzz with the news of his exceptional genius and he was compelled to take a hurried departure lest such a natural talent should become tainted by formalised tuition.

I felt in mortal fear of losing my simplicity of execution and originality of thought . . . [for] I always believed that honest originality – not eccentricity, mind you – must be the principal quality in a true artist.

He wandered south to Spain, Tangier and Malta, where the Duchess of Edinburgh, whose husband was then in command of the Mediterranean fleet, bought two of his canvases – 'Naturally, after royal patronage [she was the Tsar's daughter], I was able to double, even treble, my prices, high enough already' – then to Cairo ('I was disappointed in the Sphinx'), back to England, and off to America.

The Statue of Liberty was also a disappointment but America did him proud. As the grandson of a literary figure who was quite as celebrated in New York as in London, and as a portraitist who had enjoyed royal patronage, he was immediately in great demand. He stayed with the artist John La Farge, dined with President Harrison, mingled with the writers Kate Fields and Frances Hodgson Burnett (*Little Lord Fauntleroy*) and with the actresses Lily Langtree and Mrs Brown Potter, and painted, amongst many, the granddaughter of Abraham Lincoln. The extraordinary facility with which he could produce in a single one-hour sitting a likeness which took most artists several weeks recommended him to busy and brash tycoons. Commissions poured in. He was at last able to pay his way and, sketching busily, he progressed west to Chicago and then along the Canadian Pacific Railroad to Vancouver and a ship to Japan. 'I was craving to see something uncontaminated by Western Civilisation.'

He spent the winter of 1888/9 painting Japanese dignitaries – including the Prime Minister's family – and sketching the country's sights. Charmed with the novelty of his situation he even experimented with cultural adaptation; he quickly picked up the language and occasionally sat on the floor. Then 'the nomad spirit came upon me'. It was not Western civilisation that he wanted to break away from but all civilisation. He crossed to the northern island of Hokkaido and with ponies, cameras and canvases 'off I went, absolutely alone' to explore the island and seek out the hairy Ainu.

The Ainu were the island's indigenous inhabitants. According to Savage Landor they attacked most visitors and ate some. They were also said to be covered in hair from head to foot and therefore possible candidates for 'the missing link'. The inverted commas were his own. He, of course, made no such claims. As a scrupulously honest field-worker he merely measured and painted them. Their arms were found to be abnormally extended and their hair indeed long and abundant. One creature, a dumb lunatic who 'laboured under the impression that he was a wild bear', actually had crows feeding off the vermin in his furry coat; come spring, they might well nest there. The man lived alone in an uncommonly dirty hut and was undoubtedly deranged since he completely failed to appreciate his visitor's good intentions. 'I departed from his dwelling with a large bruise in my chest from a stone flung at me and almost minus two joints of a finger which he bit when I was trying to take anthropometric measurements of his cranium.'

Generally the Ainu were well disposed and highly appreciative of his painting. Only once did they suspect that the hobbits with which he invariably peopled his sketches were

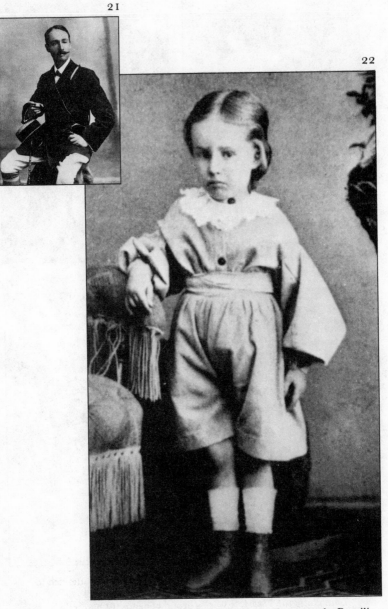

21   'I make no difference in my attire between the Brazilian
forest and Piccadilly, London.' Savage Landor dressed for
the world's wild places
22   The explorer aged 4. Arnold Henry Savage Landor

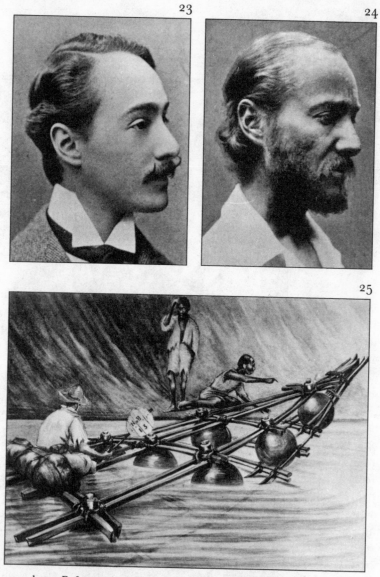

23 and 24 Before and After: mugshots of Savage Landor intended to
authenticate his sufferings at the hands of Tibetan torturers
25 Launching the *Victory*. 'I was as proud of her as if I had built a
Dreadnought'

not imaginary beasts but themselves. Then they did indeed wade in with clubs and send him packing.

Without the Ainu his first narrative of exploration would have been somewhat dull. Three thousand eight hundred miles of sodden forest and misty coastline yielded only a smashed heel, a few epic battles with mosquitoes and horse flies, and a narrow escape when caught beneath cliffs by the tide. Nevertheless the book, published by John Murray, 'the king of publishers', caused, in his own words, a sensation.

All London was talking about the Ainu. Even I, for a time, among my acquaintances seem to have lost my family name and went by the nickname of 'The Ainu' or else 'The Missing Link'. I was lionised to a considerable extent, which was quite disagreeable to me.

He had returned from Japan by way of Korea, China, Australia and Florence, netting on the way Prince George of Greece, the Tsarevich of Russia, most of the Korean royal family, 'Roberts, the celebrated champion billiard player', an Australian adventurer who, though unnamed, sounds remarkably like Louis de Rougemont, and an embittered H. M. Stanley ('To my mind Stanley had made one big mistake in his life; he had stooped to answer his critics').

With a skin considerably tougher even than Stanley's, Savage Landor could brush off critics as brusquely as he did mosquitoes. Time would reveal that the favourite breeding ground of the former was in the leather upholstery of the Royal Geographical Society's despised armchairs. It was thus somewhat unfortunate that in 1893 he accepted, not without mention of the honour thus conferred, an invitation to address the Society on the subject of the hairy Ainu. In later years this lapse occasioned the somewhat lame explanation that 'the Society was in those days serious . . . ; only men who had travelled were elected as Fellows; soon after it was converted into a popular show when, to my mind, it entirely lost its prestige'.

The Society was not alone in lionising him during the early 1890s. He was also invited to Balmoral where the Queen listened spellbound to his tales and inspected his drawings of

Hokkaido's hobbits. All doors, seemingly, were open to the intrepid traveller, and in his autobiography the pitter-patter of dropping names now becomes a thunderous downpour. Prince Henry of Battenberg, Princess Beatrice, Princess Louise, the Empress Eugenie, the Duchess of Albany, the Tsarevich (again) and the Duke of York all pleaded to hear his stories. So did T. P. O'Connor, Nellie Melba and Justin McCarthy. His paintings were no less popular and drew gasps of envy from, amongst others, James McNeill Whistler.

'Good God,' Whistler is reported to have 'exclaimed in rapture' on seeing him sketch a skull. 'It is simply wonderful. ' How on earth did you manage to get it so quickly and so correctly? It is beautiful . . . simply wonderful. If I could only draw like that I would be a great painter.' Graciously, he let Whistler keep the sketch; in return, Whistler presented him with a copy of *The Gentle Art of Making Enemies*.

Although a London exhibition of his paintings came in for some harsh words from 'men who were supposed to be connoisseurs' he cared little. The Royal Academy, in the persons of its secretary and president, was behind him and 'paid me compliments which', he sagely noted, 'would have turned the heads of most people'.

In 1896 it was the Academicians who threw a farewell dinner for him. He was off to Tibet on the journey which would make his reputation as both indomitable explorer and incorrigible fibster.

Excoriating the author of *In the Forbidden Land* is both irresistible and easy. As an artist Savage Landor had pretensions; as a writer he had none. Yet by as much as his pictures fall well short of the extravagant claims made for them, so does his prose fail to live up to even his modest disclaimers. When not downright obnoxious it has all the marks of clumsy and hurried compilation unredeemed by either the explorer's careful observations or the artist's original perceptions, or even the impostor's beguiling charm. If the genre of nineteenth-century travel writing has a nadir, this must be it.

But to be fair the fault was not entirely his own. It lay just as much with his avid readers. The more outrageous Savage Landor's claims and the more unlovable his behaviour, the more popular his books and the more elevated his reputation. *In the Forbidden Land* was a truly sensational success. It was translated into practically every European language; and its author was invited to address the Scottish, German, French and Italian Geographical Societies as well as making a much acclaimed lecture tour of the United States. If in London the Royal Geographical Society cold-shouldered him, an exhibition of his Tibetan paintings was patronised by almost the entire royal family including the Prince of Wales (Edward VII), the Duke of York (George V) and the Duchess of York (Princess May from his Florence days). The controversies which should have marked the demise of his ambitions as a credible traveller in fact promoted them. After the publication of *In the Forbidden Land* he never looked back and confounded his critics not so much by ignoring them as by outdistancing them. During the next fifteen years he seems never to have spent more than ten consecutive weeks in the same place.

In 1899 he was back on the Indo-Tibetan frontier, equipped not only with cameras and instruments but also with 'weapons, ammunitions and explosives'; this was to be 'a punitive expedition'. With a small army of recruits raised in the Indian hills he tried to slip unnoticed across the Himalayas. The plan failed. Nepalis, Tibetans (to the tune of 5,000) and British Indian forces all moved to head him off. There followed a succession of confused and ugly encounters (in which Savage Landor did terrible mischief with his rifle butt) and then a supposed crossing from Nepal into Tibet where he administered 'a sound whipping to some of those who had previously [on the last expedition] behaved so infamously'.

Having done that, I generally entertained the victims to dinner and gave them a present of money. For I ever made it a point to reward people after I had punished them as I did not want them to bear ill-feeling.

By way of rewarding the perhaps perplexed reader of *Nepal and Tibet*, the campaign ended with his putative but highly coloured ascent of Mount Lumpa (23,000 feet by his own reckoning; 16,500 according to others). Then he returned to Europe, continued west to New York and Vancouver, and reached China in time to report on the suppression of the Boxer rebellion. He joined the multi-national advance on Pekin and claims to have been the first Anglo-Saxon ever to enter the Forbidden City. Thus passed 1900.

In 1901 he again dashed through London, this time heading east across Europe and Russia. His destination was Baku on the Caspian Sea whence he embarked on a long camel trek through the deserts of Iran and Baluchistan. In 1902 he was back in London to rush out an account of the journey – *Across Coveted Lands* – and to re-equip for an immensely laborious exploration of the entire Philippine archipelago which lasted for the whole of 1903. Another book, *Gems of the East*, recounted the '16,000 miles on foot, horseback, by canoe, raft and steamer' amongst the islands, plus his heroic efforts to assist the Americans in subduing their new acquisitions and in outsmarting the Sulu Sea pirates.

By now he had been round the world three times and accumulated a fair hoard of coveted and forbidden lands. There remained the two dark continents, Africa and South America, and to reduce the time that each of them merited he resolved on two monumental transcontinental marathons that would virtually give him a clean sweep of the board. Africa was first.

The plan, for want of any worthier purpose, was to cross the continent at its widest point. 'I thought it might be interesting,' he explained. Accordingly he landed at Djibouti, faced west, and with a sizeable caravan rode and marched through Ethiopia, Sudan, Congo, Cameroon, Chad, Timbuktu and Senegal. The itinerary provided ample opportunity for those obligatory encounters with rampaging elephants ('my blood turned perfectly cold when I felt the hoarse blowing trunk of the brute only a few yards behind me'), with cannibalistic pygmies ('they were unscrupulous rascals, liars to a tantalising degree, treacherous and mean, and eaten up with personal vanity'), and with lions (although 'I never killed lions as they were too dignified and possessed such noble honest countenances'). He was again taken prisoner, this time by a Congolese chief, but the man showed little of the Tibetans' spirit and released him unharmed after only three days. All in all *Across Widest Africa* was not quite as exciting as it might have been. But it was a record.

On the very last rock of Cape Verde – and beyond as I slipped with one foot into the ocean – I ended on January 5, 1907, the longest trans-African journey which has ever been taken by white man from east to west. Two solitary bottles of champagne I had carried the entire way across widest Africa were opened on that occasion and I drank some of it in the company of two French gentlemen present. The entire journey from Djibouti had occupied 364 days, the distance covered in immense zigzags being not less than 8,500 miles. I left Africa in flourishing health and spirits, sorry that the journey had come to an end.

Three years elapsed before he was ready to tackle South America. He got side-tracked by a war in Morocco and the construction of the Panama Canal, both of which required his presence as, seemingly, did the Pope, the Italian royal family and most of Italy's aristocracy. He also found time to take up aeronautics and built, in a Paris studio, 'a new type of aeroplane' which differed from other flying machines in that it was 'not constructed to resemble a bird but rather on the principle of an arrow'.

It may be of interest to note that I was the first man to think of using twin motors and twin propellers, even before the Wright brothers had thought of using twin propellers moved by one single engine by means of bicycle chains. When I showed a photograph of my engines to Wilbur Wright he examined the picture closely, then turned almost nasty, and muttered:

'This is the only machine I have seen that I am afraid of.'

The ambiguity of Wright's comment was probably justified. The machine was shipped to Florence for trials and heard of no more. An earlier version had risen to a height of twenty feet and then nose-dived. Doubtless this new marvel of innovative design would have proved at least as disastrous. Yet the inventor's fertile mind was still busy. In 1909 he was toying with a new idea. 'Why not go to the North Pole in a submarine under the Arctic belt of ice and emerge in the supposedly open Polar Sea?' Alas, funds were not forthcoming. An aeroplane was within the scope of his pocket but not a submarine. And there was a problem with the crew; no one seemed willing to volunteer. The idea, like many others, fell by the wayside – 'perhaps it was fortunate'; South America took its place.

On January 9, 1910, he landed at Rio de Janeiro with £7,000 in cash (much of it 'good English gold') distributed about his person and a lot of shiny tin trunks. They contained £2,000 worth of equipment for 'astronomical, meteorological, photographic, anthropometric, and surveying work, also all necessary implements for constructing boats, rafts, temporary bridges, cutting roads etc., twelve first rate repeating rifles, excellent automatic pistols, and several thousand rounds of ammunition'. Only on personal gear had he economised; to wander for months in the jungles of South America he required, as in Africa, only 'comfortable suits such as I wear in Paris or London'.

This time the plan was not to cross the continent at its widest point since this would have been too easy – from Recife to Belém and then straight up the Amazon by steamer. Instead he favoured a diagonal line north-west over the entire Mato Grosso to the middle Amazon and then west through Amazonia to Peru and the Andes. He would be breaking, if not records, at least new ground since the whole interior was, he claimed, 'absolutely terra incognita'.

The first leg – to Goiaz in the vicinity of the modern Brasilia – was straightforward. He travelled in a special coach laid on by Brazilian Railways as far as Sao Paulo and then north, sitting in front of the engine to enjoy the view, across Minas Geraes to Araguari and the railhead. Here he fell out with the Chief of Police, 'a murderous-looking creature' who challenged him to a duel then reneged on the challenge; but he made friends with a German. The latter supplied him with horses and mules for the ride to Goiaz and also furnished two men. Originally he had besought the Brazilian army for an officer and a small detachment of soldiers. When these were not forthcoming, he had advertised. Still there were no takers. Brazilians were evidently a nation of cowards and he thus counted himself lucky to acquire the two Araguari men. One was a negro 'of boisterous nature' but very courageous and the other 'an anarchist with a violent revolutionary character' but even more brave. It will be remembered that Savage Landor was something of a connoisseur of brave men. As he observed, any companion of his had to be brave.

The threesome reached Goiaz after crossing five hundred kilometres of rough terrain memorable only for the ugliness of its scant mestizo population. He had never seen such sullen, sickly and surly specimens of humanity. 'Chicken-like chests' and rickety legs bespoke their depravity. Hair sprouted from about their puny physiques like, he thought, coarse grass on a patch of waste land; they were almost as hirsute as the Ainu. 'It has always been my experience that malformed people possess distorted brains'; but in this instance it was hard to distinguish cause and effect. They were all suffering from 'sexual insanity' but whether deformity encouraged vice or vice induced deformity he could not decide.

At Goiaz, the last outpost of civilisation, he demanded the thirty men deemed necessary for the work ahead. As usual, there were no takers. Of six criminals, released on his own cognizance from the local gaol, two immediately absconded, leaving him with just their four companions plus the two Araguari men. Thus woefully undermanned, the expedition headed off into the Mato Grosso. For reasons of his own he immediately doled out revolvers and ammunition to his men yet claimed never to carry a weapon himself. The result was predictable. After just three hours there occurred the first of an endless succession of mutinies.

My heart absolutely sank into my boots when I realised that it was my fate to travel with such contemptible imbeciles for perhaps a year longer or more, and this was only the first day! Oh, what a prospect! . . . With a great deal of patience I induced them to go on, which they eventually did with oaths and language somewhat unpleasant. Still I held firm.

Two nights later bullets came whistling about his head. He was unsure whether they were actually meant for him and so next day arranged some target practice. The men proved dismal shots. So long as they aimed straight at him he was thus confident of his safety. 'It was not so, of course, when they aimed somewhere else.'

Yet the next incident, only a week or so later, flatly belied this splendid bravado. He was tucked up in his silk pyjamas when another bullet ripped through the tent and then through the foot of his camp-bed. His life had been spared only because, as he now revealed, he always took the precaution of moving his bed once the men had retired to their hammocks.

The man had evidently aimed where he thought my head was resting. I, having turned the bed around, the bullet went just over my ankles.

Such inconsistencies were more a reflection on the casual composition of his narrative than on his character. Louis de Rougemont would never have made such a silly slip.

Soon after this second incident, the culprit 'who was never able to look me in the face again' absconded. He was now down to five men and, with none of them capable of more than menial tasks, he found himself 'fulfilling the posts of surveyor, hydrographer, cartographer, geologist, meteorologist, anthropologist, botanist, doctor, veterinary surgeon, painter, photographer, boat-builder, guide, navigator etc.'. The mules were as lazy and bad-tempered as the men, and the dogs – they had three – as lazy and faithless as the mules. The explorer's lot left much to be desired.

Weird rock formations and then the fossilised remains of a gigantic dinosaur kept the geologist busy until they encountered their first Indians. Even without reaching for his cranial callipers the anthropologist knew 'at a glance' that his suspicions about South America's Indians were right. They were not, like the North American Indians, of Mongolian origin but 'of Australoid or Papuan type' and some 'strongly Malay'. Even their languages, which he quickly mastered and heroically transcribed for posterity, contained many Malay and Polynesian words. He also averred that, contrary to every statistic ever produced by the Brazilian government, there were only a few hundred of them in existence – and most of these he alone had photographed and measured. ('We are not monkeys', one of them had indignantly declared when urged to register his strength on something called the dynamometer.)

June 2, Savage Landor's forty-third birthday, was 'not a happy day'. They were eight hundred and fifty kilometres from Goiaz and as good as lost. The men were all suffering from fever and planning to murder the cook. 'Worse luck for me his life was spared.' Food was disappearing at an alarming rate, another horse had been lost, and the mosquitoes were intolerable. 'Had I been a wise man I should now have turned back.' The men eagerly agreed. 'But I am not a wise man and I never turn back.' The men, as usual, mutinied.

Nevertheless, two weeks later, he did turn back. The mutiny – it was the sixth – had been quelled but the mutineers had taken their revenge by quietly jettisoning all the remaining food. He could go no further without obtaining new supplies and therefore turned south, reaching a place called Diamintino near the Bolivian border by the end of the month. There the four convicts again absconded. Arrangements were made for them to be replaced by the sole inmate of the Diamintino gaol but when this unfortunate wretch got wind of the proposed itinerary he bolted back to his cell and asked to be reshackled. At exorbitant cost – 15 shillings for a tin of sardines and 1 shilling each for eggs – Savage Landor restocked for an estimated six months and stormed back towards the Amazon having, he thought, established another useful principle of exploration.

> I owe the success of my expeditions to the fact that, no matter what happens, I never will stop anywhere . . . Many a disaster in exploring expeditions could certainly have been avoided had people known this secret of successful travelling. Push on at all costs – until, of course, you are actually dead.

In Diamintino no one doubted that the expedition was heading for disaster. 'But death or no death, we plunged once more into the unknown.' They struck the Arinos River and by an extraordinary piece of good fortune found an enormous canoe abandoned there by rubber collectors. It was forty-two feet long, weighed just under a ton, and had been hewn from a single, slightly bent tree, a feature 'which at once suggested infinite difficulty of steering'. Notwithstanding this design fault, which gave it the shape of a boomerang, Savage Landor was soon blaming the steersman for the collisions and groundings which punctuated their erratic progress. 'We travelled chiefly broadside, or else snake-like from one side of the river to the other.'

Two of the mutinous convicts returned in time to man the paddles and, with an ensign fluttering from the stern, the *Elfrida*, so named in honour of his sister, nosed north down a succession of cataracts, rapids, whirlpools and waterfalls worthy of the Dudh Kosi. The skipper's photographs, it is true, show only a shallow and meandering stream, its surface occasionally troubled by shelving rock below and a wayward current above. But its real drama only the artist could convey. In canvases frothing and foaming with Stygian fury he set a scene worthy of the clamorous page headings which would adorn his eventual account: 'Stupendous Vortex', 'Awe-inspiring Whirlpool', 'Danger Ahead', 'Redoubtable Waves'. In short, Savage Landor was at last getting into his stride, scaling the heights of hyperbole with a gusto not seen since his rough treatment by the Tibetans.

Each upset produced a life-and-death struggle in the raging waters. For hours on end they wrestled the canoe clear of rocks and dived into the vortices to rescue her cargo. Collapsing on the bank in utter exhaustion after one such session, what should he awake to find snuggled beside him but a twenty-foot boa constrictor. ('I was so tired that I went fast asleep again.') Nothing could touch him, neither the furtive jaguar that prowled past his tent nor the hideous crocodiles that snapped at the *Elfrida*'s ensign. At last, a really mighty waterfall. It was 'quite as big as Niagara' and although they had heard its roar from miles away, they somehow ended up paddling for their lives along its very lip.

My men in despair cried 'We are lost! we are lost!' We passed close to two projecting rocks. I quickly jumped onto one of them and held the canoe, my men hastily imitating my example. Just in time! We were only 10 or 15 yards from where the water curled over and rolled down the fall.

Somehow they reached the bank and there Savage Landor revealed his masterplan. To circumvent the waterfall they would drag the canoe up the bank and down a steep slope to the bottom of the falls. The bank, in his narrative, would become 'a hill range' and, because the canoe had to be moved on rollers, he wrote of 'constructing a railway track' over it. To his men the scheme, even in its simplest form, appeared impracticable. Brave men or no, they therefore did as they always did under such circumstances: they mutinied. Or rather, 'they took to their rifles and said they would follow a lunatic no more'.

Usually he responded to this challenge with superhuman patience plus a douceur; large doses of castor oil were particularly popular. But in this case he was in no mood for jokes. 'I inserted a clip of cartridges and, placing my watch before me, gave them five minutes to obey or be shot.' The necessary trees were quickly felled; 'by a careful application of the laws of leverage' the *Elfrida* slowly climbed 'over the range'.

Three weeks, two Niagaras, and five mutinies later, they reached the end of the Arinos River at a place called Barra de Sao Manoel. Henceforth the river became the Tapajoz and took a more easterly direction towards its confluence with the Amazon. This was the wrong way for one bent on reaching Peru and the *Elfrida* was therefore abandoned. Her skipper 'patted her on the nose' and experienced 'quite a *serrement de coeur*'.

It was mid-August. He had covered about one thousand five hundred miles and from the open plateau of the Mato Grosso had now descended under the canopy of the Amazonian rain forest. To reach Manaos and the middle Amazon other than by boat meant carrying all those tin trunks plus food and hacking a path through the vegetation. Only a madman would have considered it; only Savage Landor would have attempted it. With three extra porters the expedition duly staggered off into the forest.

'I carried the heaviest load of all in order to give a good example'; but example was not enough. It took the men, trailing behind him, just four days to dump the food which was supposed to last three months. Then they announced that they were returning to San Manoel. He promised castor oil, he threatened grape shot; all to no avail. Only the Araguari negro and two others broke ranks and agreed to go on. The dissidents were left in charge of the baggage and were given three tins of sardines to be getting on with. He took the other three – there were only six left – they tossed for a tin of anchovies, and the expedition broke up. It was September 1.

On the night of September 2 one of his three remaining followers tried to knife him. Fortunately he was expecting it. 'I jumped up and administered him a potent blow in the chest with the butt of my rifle.' Next day the man departed. They finished the last tin of sardines – 'our share, three and a half each'.

September 4   We travelled over five successive ranges of hills. Went twenty kilometres. Nothing to eat all day.
September 5   Another terrible march over broken country. No food.
September 6   Went over eight hill ranges with deep ravines. No food.
September 7   My men were exhausted. At night a terrific storm added to our sufferings. Ants completely ate up the upper part of my shoes. Only the heavy soles remained. With bits of string I tried to convert them into sandals but they were not a success and I flung them away. No food.

On the 8th they opened the tin of anchovies; it contained nothing but salt. There were fish in the rivers but they could find no bait. 'I was starving, barefooted and miserable'; yet round his waist he still carried £4,000 in gold. On the 9th a jaguar pawed him awake. It was standing on its hind legs, sniffing his face and gently rocking his hammock. Although his companions seemed to be hallucinating, he definitely was not.

By the 13th 'all wish for food had disappeared' and his memory – never, it will be remembered, very reliable – was playing tricks. He could not recall what country he was in and he thought his hammock was a bath; either that or the rain was continually filling it up.

That day too I fainted. When I awakened I felt my face sore. The skin of my entire left cheek and the lower eyelid had been eaten by ants. But had it not been for the incessant torture they inflicted upon us every time we fell, we should have perhaps lain there and never got up again.

On the 15th they reached the River Secunduri. Big rivers were the highways of Amazonia and on them there was always a chance of meeting with wandering rubber collectors. They therefore clung to the river, staggering along its bank in a haze of exhaustion. On the 18th they found a cassava root, ate it, were violently sick, and passed out. Next day they found more cassava and a hut. They were again very ill. Savage Landor's bare feet were riddled with thorns and jiggers and he was passing blood. He could walk no more. The hut was bare save for a number of bulbous and empty glass demijohns. Was it luck? – or licence? They were common, he explained, throughout Brazil for carrying liquor in. 'I at once conceived the idea of using them as floats in the construction of a raft.'

Dismantling part of the hut and using vines for ropes he lashed together a triangular platform resting on nine demijohns. In his weakened condition the work took two days, but the result was well worth it. 'I was as proud of her as if I had built a Dreadnought.' He christened her the *Victory*. She even floated though, laden, she slipped shyly a few inches below the surface. Without quite intending it he had realised that dream of building his own submarine.

They pushed off into the current, a curious sight consisting of three men paddling furiously across the water but without a visible boat. All went well until one of the demijohns struck a rock. It cracked and filled with water giving the *Victory* a heavy list to port. Another demijohn went and they slid even lower into the water; it was up to their armpits and still rising. Too weak to swim, too lame to walk, and too sick to posture, Savage Landor, the raconteur par excellence, decided it was time to call on the cavalry. Sure enough, just as the *Victory* went down, round the next bend came a jolly flotilla of rubber boats.

The men were saved, the hero was vindicated, justice was done. A wondrous recovery found him returning to relieve the men who had stayed behind, recover his precious baggage, and sail serenely in a well-appointed launch down the Tapajoz and then the Amazon to Santarém. There he paid off all his followers and bought a passage on an Amazon steamer –

precisely what he had planned not to do – up to Manaus. For another six months he progressed round South America; but never again did he venture from the beaten track. His exploring days were over.

Across Unknown South America is the largest and handsomest of Savage Landor's works. Writing it and 'working up' his surveys took a whole year. The map of the Arinos river alone was thirty yards long and, since he chose to name each of its myriad islands after an acquaintance, read rather like the index to *Who's Who*. He was uncommonly proud of the whole lavish production and not therefore at all surprised when an invitation arrived from Paris to give a lecture at the Sorbonne.

This was indeed a glittering occasion which he rightly saw as the pinnacle of his career. In the chair was Paul Deschanel, then President of the Chamber of Deputies. The audience included the President of the Republic, the Ministers of War, the Navy and Foreign Affairs, and the ambassadors of all the major powers. There too were a formidable array of French explorers and geographers. 'All Paris came.' Six thousand people packed into the auditorium and a further four thousand were left clamouring outside.

Speaking in French, *l'Explorateur Anglais* held this vast concourse spell-bound for two and a half hours. 'Not one single person budged . . . So absorbed was the crowd that when I ceased speaking they remained as if in a trance for several seconds. Then the applause thundered for a long time.' The President of the Chamber of Deputies could not thank him enough. Monsieur Savage Landor's bravery knew no bounds.

'"He goes without weapons, with a handful of native servants. He braves everything – hunger, thirst, malarial fevers, impenetrable forests, venomous insects, snakes, wild beasts. In serving humanity he flees from its mean-ness, passions and jealousy. Ah, Sir, you have taken of life its best part."' More thunderous applause. He was the toast of the city and was promptly signed up for a repeat performance before an audience of ten thousand at the Trocadero. 'But war broke out before the appointed date and it never came off.'

The war was a mixed blessing. It curtailed his junketing but it also saved his bacon. As usual, a number of people were none too happy about the extravagant claims made in *Across Unknown South America*. Foremost amongst these was President Theodore Roosevelt who had once had the pleasure of meeting Savage Landor and who had just published a book about his own travels in the Amazon. Though himself not averse to a bit of bravado, Roosevelt took strong exception to Savage Landor's claims to have been anywhere 'unknown' and frankly accused him of fabrication.

So did a host of Brazilians. Brazil's armed forces resented being accused of cowardice in refusing to furnish him with an escort, the country's scientists resented being accused of ignorance in respect of the Indians, not to mention the geology and geography, of the Mato Grosso, and, most of all, Brazilian travellers resented being treated as if they did not exist. The time had come when a conceited Englishman's ignorance of a distant land did not automatically make it a 'terra incognita'.

But it took that prestigious occasion at the Sorbonne to bring the critics out into the open. Suddenly the French press sensed that they were being hoodwinked by an English impostor and that here, perhaps, was a chance to get even with the English press for its rough treatment of de Rougemont. In numerous articles Savage Landor was accused of 'une série inépuisable de péripéties fantaisistes' and 'dangers imaginaires et absolument invraisemblables'. His geographical observations were about as valuable as those of Jules Verne; his 'unknown South America' was unknown only to himself.

Le Matin was particularly pleased to announce that a member of the Brazilian Academy was willing to wager 100,000 francs on the matter. If a jury, jointly selected by the French and Brazilian Geographical Societies, could find any trace of 'real scientific value' in Savage Landor's explorations, the Brazilian would make over the money; half of it was to go to establish a geographical prize and the other half to the poor of Paris. If they could not find anything of the sort, Savage Landor, as an English gentleman, would surely be willing to make a similar donation.

He was not. Indeed he refused to acknowledge the challenge. He announced that he was taking a well-deserved holiday and expected it to last ten years. Nevertheless, disgrace seemed inevitable and, had it not been for the timely end of the Archduke in Sarajevo, Savage Landor might well have received his come-uppance.

In wartime old scores were forgotten. Savage Landor dashed round Europe covering the various fronts and making his own, supposedly vital, contribution to the war effort. This consisted of a number of unusual inventions including 'two types of improvised armoured car, a new type of rigid airship, a device for destroying barbed wire entanglements, and an armoured motor-cycle with machine gun'.

Whether it was one of his own inventions which knocked him down as he got off the bus in Whitehall on the night of August 4, 1920 is unknown. He only says that it was 'a 50hp automobile travelling at 20 mph'. He was severely maimed but refused hospitalisation and was in intense pain for two weeks. 'Then I recovered.' He embarked on his autobiography, surely one of the most outrageous books ever published. He lived just long enough to finish it and died on Boxing Day 1924.

Few travellers had a better claim to having swept the board and few indeed could claim intimate acquaintance with all the crowned heads of Europe, several American presidents, Swinburne, Whistler, the Wright brothers, Sarah Bernhardt, H. M. Stanley and, of course, the hairy Ainu. Savage Landor had had a remarkable innings. But so embellished and exaggerated were his stories that the facts and achievements on which they were based were themselves called into question. He had, very nearly, been 'everywhere'. But by making *Everywhere* the title of his book he immediately roused the suspicions of any critical reader. Inadvertently, and repeatedly, he managed to discredit every undertaking in a life which, nevertheless, did indeed have 'adventures enough to fill the lives of twenty men'.

26 'Stupendous vortex'. The Elfrida and crew in the Arinos rapids

27

29

27–29 A life of vagabondage. Isabella Eberhardt dressed as a boy in 1894, in 1897 and in 1904, the year of her death, aged 27. 'I regret nothing and desire nothing. I wait'

EPILOGUE
SANDS OF PERDITION
Isabelle Eberhardt

Ain Sefra lies two hundred miles south of Oran beside Algeria's Saharan frontier with Morocco. In 1904 it consisted of a cubist jumble of crumbling mud walls and flat roofs beside a stony wadi. Over the wadi stood a bridge and under it there sometimes flowed a little water which drained from the southern slopes of the Ksour mountains, an eastern extension of the Atlas. Mostly, though, the desert claimed these waters long before they reached Ain Sefra. The town relied on its wells (*ain* means 'a well'), and the wadi stayed dry, sprouting grass and scrub close-cropped by the town's goats.

It also offered a short cut to the Redoute. Here, on rising ground across the wadi, the French had established a military headquarters. In 1904, with the pacification of the Sud-Oranais well in hand and the absorption of Morocco about to begin, the Redoute swarmed with uniforms and horses. Its bugle calls vied with the Ain Sefra muezzin and from its tented lines legionnaires would slip across the wadi to sample Ain Sefra's civilian distractions.

On the morning of October 21, soon after nine o'clock, the legionnaires were in the mess having breakfast. It was a fine clear day but with the heat already sapping its promise. Below the Redoute the goatherds were out with their flocks; Ain Sefra buzzed with domestic activity. Then came a rumbling sound. To Slimene Ehnni, a visitor to the town, it was like the noise made by a convoy of lorries. People began running and shouting. He lent over the balcony of his rented room. 'The wadi,' they were screaming, 'the wadi.' Then he saw the flood. A boiling avalanche of mud and masonry and goats and trees, *café-au-lait*-coloured, was boring down the wadi. 'It rose up like a wall; it raced like a stampeding horse; it was at least two metres high.' It snatched at the walls and sucked at the houses.

I saw the danger and we fled [Slimene Ehnni later recalled]. The torrent caught us. I do not know how I escaped. My wife was carried away.

Up on the Redoute officers and men watched horror-struck as the bridge went down and then the whole of the lower part of the town seemed to slip into the flood. Someone recognised the garrison's postman marooned on his roof top and a trooper swam to the rescue; both were swept under. It was afternoon before the waters began to subside and midnight before a crossing could be effected.

Next day the garrison turned out to help in the salvage work. A temporary bridge was erected and channels dug to drain the standing water; far out into the desert bodies were being prised from the mud. Thirty were brought in but of Slimene Ehnni's wife there was no sign.

Mystified, Colonel Lyautey despatched a trusted officer to lead the search. More than Ehnni himself, Lyautey, the man who was masterminding operations against Morocco and would soon emerge as France's most distinguished and enlightened colonialist, was deeply troubled. For in Slimene Ehnni's wife he mourned the loss of a valued agent. As Si Mahmoud, an Islamic scholar, she – or in this case, he – had discharged himself from the military hospital only the day before. Lyautey mourned, too, the loss of a close friend, possibly a lover; for Si Mahmoud or Mme Slimene Ehnni was also Isabelle Eberhardt, Arabist and voluptuary. Above all he mourned the loss of one who, however baffling, absurd and irresponsible, was like himself of independent mind, a true 'original', a free spirit.

At last, ignoring the husband's testimony, the searchers began to probe the ruins of the house in which the couple had been staying. There, crushed beneath rocks, timbers and mud, they found the thin ravaged body. It lay limp and sated as if the searing pangs of lust and, latterly, pain had been finally doused by the flood. But whatever charms and whatever strength it had once possessed had also been wasted by malaria and syphilis, alcohol and hashish. The head was shaven, the gums rotted, the teeth gone. It was the corpse of a crone. To Lyautey, as to others, it seemed that death had been merciful in its timing. Only life had been cruel. It had taken its terrible toll of 'poor Mahmoud' in just twenty-seven years.

Lyautey himself took charge of her obsequies. He saw to it that she was buried in a Muslim cemetery and according to Islamic law. A verse from the Koran was inscribed on her gravestone. Then he salvaged what papers had survived the flood and sent them off to Algiers. Edited and embroidered, often beyond recognition, the writings of Isabelle Eberhardt began to appear soon afterwards. A life which at the time the French *colons* had found impossibly sordid and irresponsible rapidly became a romantic legend. 'The Amazon of the Sands', they called her, 'La Bonne Nomade', 'Isabella of Africa', 'The Desert Cossack'.

She herself, though nothing if not a romantic, had been content to describe her life as one of 'vagabondage'. She used a frugal vocabulary and chose her words with care; 'vagabondage' was no exception. The notion of a nomadism that was both compulsive and delinquent was precisely what she meant.

I regret nothing and desire nothing. I wait. A nomad with no other homeland than Islam, without family or confidants, alone, forever alone in the solitude of my soul, I will travel my road through life until the time comes for the great eternal sleep of the grave.

'Mekhtoub', she often added, 'it is written'; nothing could change it; no one could reform her. It was her destiny to explore the frontiers of the soul, to wander in forbidden lands between the womb and the void.

Her life was a succession of journeys but none of them conforms to the pattern of others related in this book. For Isabelle Eberhardt, in life as in her writings, the experience of the moment counted for everything. Like photos snapped at random, scenes of no consequence alternate with incidents of drama and poignancy. But each seems unconnected, as fortuitous as that final flash flood in the desert. Though faithfully observed and vividly described, they are linked by no narrative, only by the outpourings of a tortured soul. The solitude of the desert is but a mirror of her own solitude; melancholy, like malaria, comes in long feverish bouts.

Most romantic travellers are content to romanticise their travels; their homes and their families can be utterly mundane. But Isabelle Eberhardt claimed no home. Her whole life was one continuous journey and it was her whole life that she romanticised. In anyone else such indulgence would be either insufferable or hilarious; in her case it was simply tragic.

Born into an eccentric emigré family living in the limbo of Geneva, she began life with a question mark after her name, her father, her nationality, and even her sex. Only her mother, a shadowy and vulnerable presence whom she always referred to as 'The White Spirit', was beyond dispute. She was Mme Nathalie de Moerder, the illegitimate daughter of a wealthy Jew and the wife of a Russian aristocrat, General Paul de Moerder. In 1871, having borne him three children, she eloped with the man who had been engaged as their tutor. Taking the children, the couple fled to Turkey and then to Switzerland where a fourth child, Augustin, who may or may not have been the General's, was born.

Her fifth, born in 1877, was named (not christened) Isabelle Wilhelmine Marie Eberhardt. The surname was borrowed from Nathalie de Moerder's mother, presumably a German. Logically the tutor, Alexander Trophimovsky, should have been the father. But he never acknowledged Isabelle and she never acknowledged him. Her only mention of her real father would be that he had died a Muslim – a claim which, unless it was sheer fantasy, precludes the free-thinking tutor. Armenian by birth and at one time a priest in the Orthodox Church, Alexander Trophimovsky had undergone a dramatic change of heart, been defrocked, and was now an atheist, anarchist and nihilist at war with society, religion, art and just about everything except science. It could be that he rejected paternity in the same iconoclastic spirit; that would explain why Isabelle was surnamed Eberhardt.

But it does not account for her other names. A French biographer with no hard evidence but a wealth of circumstantial detail has suggested that her real father was in fact the poet Arthur Rimbaud. He was in Switzerland at the appropriate time, his favourite sister was called Isabelle, and to Queen Wilhelmina of the Netherlands he owed his chance to serve with the Dutch forces and so fulfil his dream of visiting Java. More to the point, Isabelle Eberhardt looked exactly like Rimbaud, was of the same build, shared the same melancholic view of life and was equally fascinated by Islam. And Rimbaud did indeed die a Muslim. Most extraordinary of all, in her writings Isabelle Eberhardt would adopt themes, attitudes and even phrases so similar to some of Rimbaud's that they 'amount to plagiarism' – yet there was no evidence that she had ever read him.

If far from convincing, the 'parallèlisme' is certainly instructive. For one cast as a 'rimbaudienne' dreamer it is hard to conceive of a worse fate than an upbringing at the hands of Trophimovsky the ex-priest. In a large secluded villa with an overgrown garden that was almost an estate the tyrannical tutor presided over a succession of bizarre experiments in market gardening and exotic horticulture. An admirer of Tolstoy, he dragooned the children into tending his plantations whilst preaching to them of the dignity of labour and the principles of the commune. The only formal education that his extreme views permitted him was in languages. He taught the children Greek, Latin, Arabic, French, German and Italian – then followed his lessons with corrective outbursts designed to countervail any unhealthy tendencies towards normality which their polyglot reading might induce.

In effect, the children, like the cactus garden, the market garden, and the trout farm, were grandly conceived experiments and all equally doomed to failure. As the tyrant lurched from one crazy venture to the next, the chaotic house filled with foreboding and intrigue. Neighbours shied away in horror; the only visitors were furtive Russian revolutionaries; and as Trophimovsky vented his frustration with instructive denunciations like 'Jesus Christ is a bastard', 'the White Spirit' cowered behind the samovar and the children dreamt of escape.

It was Trophimovsky who decided that Isabelle should dress as a boy. At seventeen, as she faced the camera of a local photographer, she wore naval uniform, at eighteen she was dressed as a Turk, and at nineteen as a fanciful Bedouin. Like the 'after' shot to these 'befores' there is also a picture of her taken just before her death; two small hands (one with cigarette) and a bald head peek from voluminous burnous and turban. There are no known photos of her in female attire and it seems that what began as an imposition soon became a habit. It was more convenient to wear men's clothes and they suited her physique. Like a pot plant with a mutilated root system, the androgynous teenager in the sailor suit failed to develop the shapely curves and stately cleavage of womanhood. Her hips stayed narrow, her breasts small. She spoke with a whining nasal drawl and walked with a slouch. For once a Trophimovsky experiment in exotic horticulture had worked.

But fashions change. At the time most men of her own race found her physique repulsive, even depraved. Only Arabs, it was suggested, with their supposed ambi-sexual inclinations, could possibly see her as an object of pleasure. Nowadays *gamin* charms, a sensual mouth and an air of sexual mystery command attention. Much of her posthumous celebrity may be traced to our fascination with boyish insouciance and the pubescent figure.

In 1897, with one of those abrupt changes of scene so typical of her life, the twenty-year-old Isabelle and her mother took off for Algeria. Escape from Trophimovsky and the gloomy villa had become a family obsession. One of the de Moerder boys had absconded to Russia, another was about to commit suicide, the only de Moerder girl had run off with a local shopkeeper, and Augustin, the youngest of the boys and Isabelle's sweetheart, had eluded his creditors, Tsarist agents and Trophimovsky by enrolling in the French Foreign Legion. Now he was regretting his decision and apparently thinking of returning to Geneva. It was to dissuade him from doing anything so foolish – and to get away themselves – that Isabelle and the 'White Spirit' descended on North Africa.

In this new land of white light and sparkling dust Isabelle immediately recognised her proper environment. As children she and Augustin had pored over the romances of Pierre Loti, the French sailor turned prolific writer and lover whose exotic imagery and atmospheric style were much in vogue. From Loti, from her Arabic studies, and from occasional Muslim visitors, Isabelle had formed romantic notions of Islam and the Arabs. She had made pen friends with a French officer serving in Algeria and had exchanged pseudonymous letters with several Muslim divines. What amounted to a correspondence course in Islamic studies may have been just a reaction to the hateful anaemia of Geneva and the atheistic rantings of Trophimovsky; but in Algeria it bore fruit. Mother and daughter settled in Bône (Annaba) not amongst the French *colons* but in the native city; Isabelle adopted the burnous and turban; and within a few weeks she and her mother had both formally converted to Islam.

For Nathalie de Moerder, the half-Jewish wife of a Russian general and the mistress of an Armenian atheist, becoming a Muslim must have been the ultimate gesture of protest. But for her, and especially for Isabelle Eberhardt, the determinism of Islam had its appeal. The world of *mekhtoub* (it is written) and *Inshallah* (God willing) subsumed that mixture of Slavic fatalism and Calvinist predestination to which they had been accustomed in Geneva. A sense of submission to destiny fulfilled a deep-felt need and tallied with Isabelle's romantic ideal. Pierre Loti, according to his biographer, 'was born to travel, to love, and to write; he knew his destiny and he accepted it'. In almost identical words Isabelle Eberhardt, now calling herself Si Mahmoud (the same name, incidentally, as that of Loti's favourite Algerian), described her life in Bône at this time.

I study the Quran and I write. But my ambition to make a name for myself with the pen (something in which I have little confidence and do not seriously expect to achieve) is secondary. I write because I like the mechanics of literary creation; I write, as I love, because it is my destiny.

Her writings consisted of a Loti-esque diary full of soul-searching sighs and plaintive sketches plus a few short stories. To the diary she committed some of her anguish when in late 1897 her mother, now called Fatima but still referred to as 'the White Spirit', died of a heart attack. 'How can I sustain any illusions when the white dove who was the sweetness and light of my life is sleeping out there in the earth?' Trophimovsky, in Algiers for the funeral, consoled her by handing her his revolver; she had made the mistake of saying that she wished she could still be with her mother. Augustin, meanwhile, had left the Foreign Legion and retired to Marseilles, there to marry a French woman whom Isabelle always called the 'ouvrière', the factory-girl. For the first time she was well and truly 'seul, toutement seul'. With what money her mother had left her she bought a horse and began the wanderings that were to last the rest of her life.

In 1898 she was in Tunis, living in the casbah and scandalising the European community by frequenting hashish dens and disreputable coffee houses. She drank *anis* and smoked incessantly. 'When she wanted a man she took him,' recalled a French resident, 'she'd beckon and off they'd go.' It was rumoured that she was a wealthy Russian Jewess and that her eccentricities might be intended to disguise political intrigues of some sort. She was therefore watched. In the following year she was again in Tunis and then made a wide sweep through the desert by way of El Oued and Toggourt back to Bône. The oasis township of El Oued with its domed houses set amidst a sea of dunes 'far from men and their baseness' became her goal and in late 1900, with a dubious private commission to look for a lost French explorer, she again set off south into the Sahara.

Last night I slept on the ground beside a fire of dry brush, lying on the warm sand looking up at the countless stars. Oh Sahara, menacing Sahara, hiding your beautiful soul in inhospitable and mournful solitude. I love this country of sand and stones, this land of camels and simple people, this land of salt lakes and sculptured dunes.

In El Oued she rented a house with a courtyard and settled down for six months. It was her intention to rekindle her Islamic fervour and to write. Although she must have undergone some Qur'anic instruction it was the esoteric and mystical side of Islam which excited her. Then as now North Africa was deeply impregnated with Sufism. Muslims – Berber or Arab – belonged to one or other of the major Sufi sects and revered a host of marabouts, sheikhs, or khalifas, living and dead, whose precepts they followed and whose *baraka*, or spiritual power, they invoked for miraculous purposes. For Si Mahmoud, who was initiated into the Qadriya order soon after her arrival in El Oued, *baraka* was less about miracle working than about mystical communion. In the trance-like ecstasy induced by abstinence, meditation, *dhikr* (ritual chant and dance), and sometimes drugs, the initiate might expect to experience a direct knowledge of God.

The brotherhoods were also immensely influential social and political organisations – a fact that was not lost on the French authorities. As a Qadriya, Si Mahmoud was making a commitment to the Arabs as well as to Islam. But although she bitterly criticised French attitudes towards their subjects, there is no evidence that she engaged in political intrigue. For the local Qadriya sheikh she acted as a part-time translator and secretary; and amongst the Sahara's nomadic shepherds she prescribed in the name of the Qadriyas. That was all. She was simply doing what Mary Kingsley would have described as 'odd jobs for Africa' in the name of Islam.

Even her disguise was patently innocent. In El Oued it was common knowledge that Si Mahmoud was in fact a European and a girl. But so obviously dedicated to her religion was this epicene waif that her co-religionists were inclined to see her eccentricity as evidence of unusual spiritual potential. A hint of maraboutic power emanated from her always dazzlingly white burnous. If she wrote a lot she must be a scholar and, to judge by her consumption of hashish, something of a dervish. At night she was seen to gallop off across the moonlit sands and to sleep amongst the dunes. She was a law unto herself; she belonged to no one. Yet on one of these nocturnal escapades she met a *spahi*, an Algerian soldier, and thereafter shared with him the mystery of the desert night and the warmth of the sands. The man was Slimene Ehnni and, perhaps because he was more vulnerable than her other lovers, perhaps because he too was hopelessly smitten, or perhaps because amongst ardent Arab lovers he was the most ardent, she drifted into an intense and lasting relationship.

The months at El Oued were not the happiest of her life for she could no more be happy than look pretty; but they were the quietest and the least bitter, 'long hours with neither sadness nor boredom' interspersed with secret assignations beneath the feathery palms.

I am beginning to believe that I have found my haven, me to whom contentment in a European town was never a possibility and to whom the thought of a harsh desert existence was an inspiration ... Everyday I become more attached to Slimene until he has become part of my family – or rather he is my family.

Slimene moved into her house in El Oued and they papered its bare mud walls with fantasies of a shared domesticity. They would buy a café; he would leave the army; she would help him with his French, he her with her Arabic.

But as the harsh desert winter set in – and as her money ran out – the idyll of 'this languid existence amongst the shifting sands' drew to a close. In early 1901 Slimene's troop was recalled to barracks near Constantine – 'anguish unutterable', wrote his lover. She was badly in debt and, in the hopes of securing a loan from her Qadriya sheikh, set off on pilgrimage with him. The sheikh's cortège stopped for the night in a village. Si Mahmoud was translating a letter for him in the courtyard of their temporary quarters when she was savagely cut down from behind.

Once again the scene abruptly changed. She was in hospital recovering from multiple injuries. Slimene was gone and she was sick and utterly alone. Her assailant was to stand trial. The colonial press were having a field-day, but neither they, nor she, nor anyone else had the faintest idea what it had all been in aid of. It was clear that the attack was premeditated and that the attacker was acting on someone else's orders. He claimed he received them direct from God, and to the extent that she too ascribed the whole affair to the will of Allah, Isabelle agreed. But he also belonged to a rival Sufi order.

Was she, then, the victim of some old anti-Qadriya vendetta? – or of anti-colonial sentiment? – or just of a lover's caprice? Fidelity was not part of her relationship with Slimene and one rumour had it that the Sheikh himself had instigated the attack to get rid of a tiresome mistress.

All this and more was hinted at during the trial. Isabelle, dressed for once as a woman, albeit an Arab woman, disclaimed all animosity towards the accused and pleaded for leniency. Ideally she would have preferred that the matter be overlooked altogether. She had survived the attack on her life but now the trial meant an assault on her character. The respectable French *colons* licked their lips over the reports of her desert amours while the authorities clucked their tongues over the possible political mischief. So long as the Russian girl had hugged the casbah walls and stayed out of the limelight they had been prepared to overlook her ambiguous behaviour. But now she was out in the open and bearing the stigma of notoriety. Might not the brotherhoods use her once again to stir up trouble? Justice must of course be done; her assailant therefore received a life sentence. But she too could not go free; as she left the court she was handed an expulsion order.

In hospital, between logging the spasms of her severed muscles, she had written bitterly of her shattered dreams. 'There is no rest anywhere. I can't go on. A terrible agony has taken possession of my soul and helpless childish tears roll down my cheeks.' Without the resignation enjoined by Islam and the consolation of her diary she would have been the third of Nathalie de Moerder's children to commit suicide. The desert had lost its charm; even its emptiness she now found dull. But life in the city, as she awaited the trial, was no better. She had to report to the police every day; she lived on charity and cigarettes. Only Slimene, with whom she was able to snatch a few hours whenever he could get leave, gave her reason to live and to hope.

Because expulsion meant separation from Slimene she protested. She insisted that her behaviour, however unconventional, had been in keeping with her faith and of no possible political significance. In an impressively level-headed appeal that actually won her some sympathy, she quoted the head of the Arab Bureau in El Oued who had vouched for her. He still had nothing with which to reproach her other than that she was 'an original'. She explained:

I am not a politician; I am the agent of no party; I am nothing but a thinker and a dreamer who wants to live a free and nomadic life and to try to communicate to others a little of the melancholy charm one experiences in the face of the splendours of the Sahara.

In her bid to lead a life free of both physical and social constraints she had come to identify travel with trauma and observation with experience. Forbidden lands meant forbidden pleasures; and the journey of the soul was the journey of the senses. In this she seems to anticipate a later generation of expatriot seekers and to belong amongst the lotus eaters of Bali or on the Indian ashram circuit.

Yet that desire to communicate her experience, to write, was also genuine. The blow of her expulsion was softened by the news that an Algerian newspaper had accepted some of her short stories. And at Augustin's home in Marseilles, where she now took refuge, she began work on a novel. Her sketches of desert life are filled with simple vivid detail. The dune-comber of El Oued wrote, as she loved, knowing that it was not just her destiny but also her forte. Had she lived long enough to digest her experiences she might well have written her own *Out of Africa*.

No less genuine was her faith in Islam – she is said seldom to have missed the obligatory prayers five times a day – and this too suggests a more responsible motivation for her 'vagabond-age'. Through the obligation of *haj* (pilgrimage) Islam has ever been a powerful force in encouraging travel. Before the sixteenth century most of the great travellers were Muslims and none were more illustrious than those from the Maghreb (North Africa and Spain). Ibn Batuta, in the fourteenth century, began his world-wide peregrinations in Morocco and returned there to write his account of them. His contemporary, the historian Ibn Khaldun, wandered the byways between Tunis and Fez and back again before finally gravitating to Cairo. And in the sixteenth century the man known in

Europe as Leo Africanus also prefaced his journey into black Africa by roaming through Morocco and Algeria; and he returned to Algeria to die. The coast, the mountains, and the desert were criss-crossed by routes of trade and pilgrimage. From city to city and from shrine to shrine scholars and merchants were ever on the move, riding on horseback or walking beside their camels. Isabelle Eberhardt followed in their tracks, roaming from oasis to mosque in search of spiritual enlightenment or accompanying her sheikh on the rounds of his followers.

During her final years her itineraries would increasingly focus on places of religious retreat and instruction. But first she had to circumvent the expulsion order and regain North Africa. To this problem there was a dazzlingly simple solution – marry Slimene. As a quartermaster in the *spahis* he automatically received French citizenship; as his wife she too would become a French citizen; as a French citizen she could go wherever she pleased on French territory – which included Algeria.

Through the summer of 1901 she lobbied for Slimene's transfer to Marseilles while herself earning a few francs as a letter-writer amongst the city's North African immigrants and even for a time working in the docks. In October her efforts bore fruit. Slimene was transferred and they were married, first in Marseilles' town hall and then in its mosque. For the occasion she wore a skirt (a black one), a lilac blouse, a black wig and a black hat trimmed with lilacs. It was by way of a concession to Slimene for whom these things mattered. His part of the bargain was to leave the army. With his demob imminent they returned to Algeria in January 1901.

At last the dream of our return has come true. We are once more in the eternal and youthful sunlight of this beloved land. This is indeed the start of our new life and of the joy for which we have long yearned and surely deserve. Knowing that the whole of the Mediterranean now distances us from that thrice-accursed Marseilles gives me an overwhelming sense of physical well-being.

Briefly the dream lived up to expectations. Slimene secured a civil appointment as secretary to the municipal administration of Ténès, midway between Algiers and Oran. Although his wife heartily detested the local expatriot community, financial pressures were somewhat relieved and she was able to concentrate on her writing. Thanks to the publicity surrounding her trial and expulsion, she was no longer dismissed as just an eccentric Russian drop-out. In Algiers Victor Barrucand, editor of *Les Nouvelles* which had protested against her treatment, now adopted her as a regular contributor to his paper and introduced her to other intellectuals sympathetic to the Arabs and critical of colonial injustices. She became an acknowledged authority on the desert peoples and on the Sufi brotherhoods. At last she had an audience indulgent towards her moods, her swearing, drinking and chain-smoking, and profoundly impressed by her experiences. With Victor Barrucand began the romantic legend which would posthumously clothe the tragic reality.

Draped in the folds of her severe burnous, her head swathed in a high turban with brown cords, booted like a military horseman, her style unequivocal, she rested on her elbow amid a heap of cushions and propounded her pet theories . . . Warming to her subject she would rise, take a few steps across the room which was open to the sea, and tap out her little pipe of *kif* [hashish]. She moved with an easy grace, tall, slim, flat-chested like an Amazon – she looked very young. Her rounded forehead shaded her penetrating gaze which contrasted strongly with her languid posture and the aristocratic pose of her hands . . . This wanderer could certainly talk to us of freedom.

Combining her work for Barrucand's paper with her compulsive 'vagabondage', she was soon absenting herself from home and husband in Ténès to roam again on the Hauts Plateaux and along the desert fringes. As usual, she chose her companion as impulsively as she chose her itinerary. The one was often faceless as the other was often placeless. What mattered, and what inspired her writing, was the experience.

The evening was clear and fresh. A great silence reigned in the desert town and we passed through like shadows, Mohammed and I. This man, so Bedouin and so close to nature, is my companion of choice because he matches the countryside so completely – as he matches the people and my own state of mind. More than that he shares, unconsciously, my preoccupation with the dark matters that trouble the senses. He wants that which I understand and he feels it even more intensely than I do simply because he doesn't understand and doesn't even want to.

Early in 1903 she was again travelling south, obsessed this time not with the dark secrets of the senses but with the no less pressing cravings of the spirit. She was going on pilgrimage to a shrine and centre of learning near Bou-Saada which was presided over by a lady marabout. The journey, in mid-winter, was arduous; when she arrived she was suffering from the first of those malarial fevers which would now punctuate her travels. Slowly she recovered, lulled by the serenity of this desert retreat with its blue domes and its mosque in which disciples maintained a continuous recitation of prayers. Although Lella Zeynab, the *maraboute*, failed to impart that sudden spiritual enlightenment that she sought, she emerged from her audiences buoyant and 'rejuvenated'. Only the melancholy of the desert oppressed her. It seemed now even heavier and more menacing. 'There is so much that is ambiguous about it, half understood, mysterious . . .'

At this point, eighteen months before her death, her published journal ends. From other sources it appears that she returned to Ténès and that later in the same year she went south again. Officially she was to report for Barrucand's paper on the military activities around Ain Sefra. But there she met Colonel Lyautey who immediately recognised that in Si Mahmoud she had a persona acceptable to the Sufi orders and therefore of great potential value in his attempts to reach a peaceful settlement in the area. Soon she was accompanying parties of legionnaires as liaison officer and helping to gather intelligence.

In 1904 came her big chance to break new ground and make her name as a political traveller. She was despatched on her own, beyond French lines, and further into the desert than ever before, with the object of winning the support of Sidi Brahim, sheikh of Kenadsa which was nominally subject to the Sultan of Fez and therefore Moroccan territory. As his guest, disciple and sometimes, it seemed, prisoner, she spent the whole summer in this remote and practically unknown desert township. The cloistered life of meditation and prayer was far stricter than amongst the Qadriyas of Algeria and it seems that here she underwent a profound spiritual reconversion. 'I bless my solitude which allows me to *believe*, which is making of me once more a simple and exceptional creature, resigned to my destiny.' In copious notes later published under the title *Dans l'Ombre Chaude de L'Islam* she recorded the daily routine behind the blank walls of an intensely conservative and ordered fraternity. She described the repressed longings of the novice-scholars in their high-ceilinged communal apartments and she evoked in telling detail the more public atmosphere of prayer and meditation in the halls and mosques. Morocco had resisted Ottoman dominion and, on the eve of the French conquest, places like Kenadsa were little changed since the days of Ibn Batuta. She was reporting not just on a remote and hidden community but on life as lived in the medieval heyday of Islam.

Sadly an attack of malaria served to bring on more twentieth-century doubts and anxieties. Death, if that was already her destiny, she accepted; but the indifference which this resignation should generate she could neither accept in others nor imitate herself. She longed for sympathy. Where was there anyone who could help her, anyone who would mourn for her?

I was alone, alone in this lost corner of Morocco, and wherever I had lived I had been alone and should remain so wherever I went, for ever . . . I had neither country, nor home, nor family. Perhaps I had not even any friends left. I had passed through life like a stranger, arousing nothing but criticism and hatred. At this moment I was suffering, far from all help, among men who would impassively watch the ruin of all around them, cross their arms in the face of illness and death, and say 'Mekhtoub'.

When she left Kenadsa she was still weak and far from well. She rode into Ain Sefra and was immediately admitted to the military hospital in the Redoute. It was from there that on October 20 she discharged herself and crossed the wadi in order to meet with Slimene who had just arrived from Ténès. They spent the night together, their last.

Isabelle Eberhardt died neither friendless nor unmourned. Slimene retired into a grief-stricken obscurity; Barrucand and her other literary friends poured forth fulsome plaudits; even the Paris papers noted her passing. But it was Lyautey, the future General, whose brutally honest assessment best conveyed the loss and the waste that was as much a verdict on her life as on her death.

Poor Mahmoud. She had reached a state of melancholy which nothing could dispel for long. Success had come too late. She did not complain but one sensed a bitter disillusionment. Although she was only twenty-seven, there was no future for her and she must have known it. I loved her for what she was and for what she was not. I loved her prodigious artistic temperament. She was truly herself – a rebel.

BIBLIOGRAPHY

CHAPTER 1

Cochrane, J. D., *A Pedestrian Journey through Russia and Siberian Tartary to the Frontiers of China, the Frozen Sea, and Kamchatka,* London, 1824 (3rd edition, London, 1829).

Cochrane, A., *The Fighting Cochranes,* London, 1983.

Horder, M., 'The Pedestrian', in *Folio Society Quarterly,* Autumn 1977.

Quarterly Review, London, December 1825.

Keay, J., *Eccentric Travellers,* London, 1983.

CHAPTER 2

MacGregor, J., *A Thousand Miles in the Rob Roy Canoe,* London, 1866.

MacGregor, J., *The Rob Roy on the Baltic,* London, 1867.

MacGregor, J., *The Voyage Alone in the Yawl 'Rob Roy',* London, 1868.

MacGregor, J., *The Rob Roy on the Jordan,* London, 1869.

Hodder, E., *John MacGregor ('Rob Roy'),* London, 1894.

MacGregor, D., *The Loss of the Kent,* nd.

CHAPTER 3

Aurousseau, M. (editor and translator), *The Letters of F. W. Ludwig Leichhardt* 3 vols, Hackluyt Society, 1968.

Leichhardt, L., *Journal of an Overland Expedition in Australia from Moreton Bay to Port Essington,* London, 1847.

Russell, H. S., *The Genesis of Queensland,* Sydney, 1888.

Cotton, C. D., *Ludwig Leichhardt and the Great South Land,* Sydney, 1938.

Chisholm, A. H., *Strange New World,* Sydney, 1941.

CHAPTER 4

Kingsley, M. H., *Travels in West Africa*, London, 1897.
Kingsley, M. H., *West African Studies*, London, 1899.
Gwynn, S., *Life of Mary Kingsley*, London, 1932.
Pedler, F., *The Lion and the Unicorn in Africa*, London, 1974.

CHAPTER 5

The Wide World Magazine, London, August 1898–May 1899.
The Daily Chronicle, London, September and October 1898.
Barton, M. and Sitwell, O., *Sober Truth*, London, 1930.
Chatwin, B., *In Patagonia*, London, 1977.

CHAPTER 6

Savage Landor, A. H., *Alone with the Hairy Ainu*, London, 1891.
Savage Landor, A. H., *In the Forbidden Land*, London, 1898.
Savage Landor, A. H., *Across Unknown South America*, London, 1914.
Savage Landor, A. H. *Everywhere*, London, 1924.
Anon. *La Récente Exploration au Brésil de M: Savage Landor* (Foreword by Armand Ledent), Paris, 1914.
Hopkirk, P., *Trespassers on the Roof of the World*, London, 1982.
Allen, C., *A Mountain in Tibet*, London, 1982.

EPILOGUE

Eberhardt, I., *Mes Journaliers*, Paris, 1923.
Eberhardt, I. (avec V. Barrucand), *Dans l'Ombre Chaude de l'Islam*, Paris, 1905.
Eberhardt, I. (avec V. Barrucand), *Notes de Route*, Paris, 1908.
Stephan, R., *Isabelle Eberhardt*, Paris, 1930.
Mackworth, C., *The Destiny of Isabelle Eberhardt*, London, 1951.
Blanch, L., *The Wilder Shores of Love*, London, 1954.
Eaubonne, F., *La Couronne de Sable*, Paris, 1968.